NORTH MACE TRAVEL GUIDE 2025

Uncover the Balkans' Best-Kept Secrets – Mountains, Heritage, and Timeless Wonders Await.

GLORIA JANE

COPYRIGHT © GLORIA JANE 2025 All rights reserved. This companion guide, including its content, design, and layout, is protected under international copyright law. No portion of this publication may be reproduced, distributed, or transmitted in any form or by any means whether electronic, mechanical, photocopying, recording, or otherwise without the prior written permission of the author. Unauthorized use or distribution of any material from this guide, including brief quotations in reviews or references, is strictly prohibited and may result in legal action. For permissions, contact the author directly. All inquiries and permissions must be granted in writing. This guide is intended solely for personal use, and any commercial exploitation is expressly forbidden unless specifically authorized by the author.

MAP

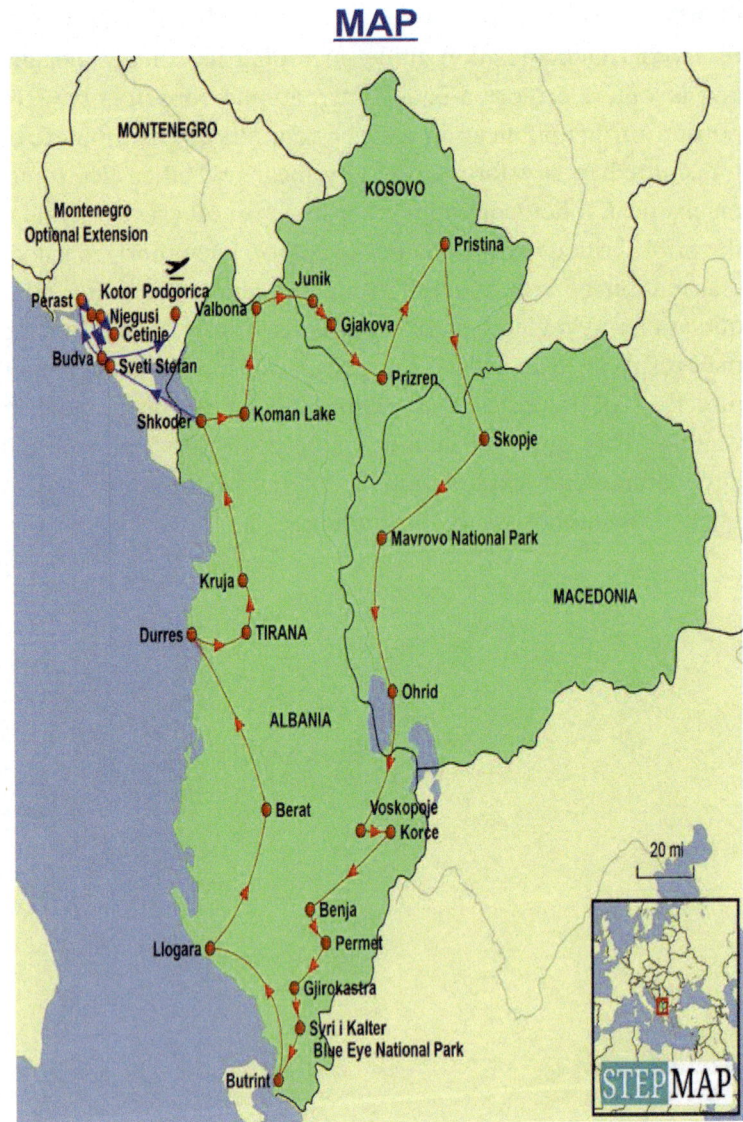

TABLE OF CONTENTS

Chapter 1: Welcome to North Macedonia
- ❖ History Of North Macedonia: lifestyle, landscape And culture
- ❖ My Travel Experience To North Macedonia
- ❖ Key Highlights and Unique Features
- ❖ Top Reasons to Visit North Macedonia
- ❖ Making Friends In North Macedonia

Chapter 2: Planning Your Trip To North Macedonia
- ❖ Entry and Visa Requirements
- ❖ Customs Rules And Regulations
- ❖ Health, Safety, and Travel Insurance
- ❖ Best Times to Visit and Seasonal Tips
- ❖ Suggested Packing List
- ❖ Budgeting Tips

Chapter 3: Getting to North Macedonia
- ❖ Major Airports and Airlines
- ❖ Tips for Border Crossings
- ❖ Overview of Flights and Common Layovers

Chapter 4: Essential Travel Information
- ❖ Currency and Exchange, Banks, and ATMs
- ❖ Language Basics and Key Phrases

- ❖ Local Laws and Customs
- ❖ Connectivity: SIM Cards, Wi-Fi, and Internet Tips

Chapter 5: Getting Around North Macedonia
- ❖ Public Transportation: Buses, Trains, and Taxis
- ❖ Car Rentals and Driving Tips
- ❖ Biking, Walking Tours, and Eco-Friendly Travel Options
- ❖ Travel Apps and Helpful Resources

Chapter 6: Top Destinations And Tourist Must-Visit Attractions
- ❖ Skopje: City Highlights and Main Sights
- ❖ Ohrid: Lake, Old Town, and UNESCO Heritage Sites
- ❖ Bitola: Historical Gems and Cultural Spots
- ❖ Mavrovo National Park and Outdoor Escapes
- ❖ Other Must-See Cities, Towns, and Villages
- ❖ Kokino Observatory
- ❖ Heraclea Lyncestis
- ❖ Stobi Archaeological Site
- ❖ Marko's Towers (Markovi Kuli)
- ❖ Tikves Wine Region

Chapter 7: Hidden Gems and Off-the-Beaten-Path Adventures
- ❖ Lesser-Known Historic Sites
- ❖ Scenic Landscapes and Natural Wonders
- ❖ Unique Local Experiences and Traditions

Chapter 8: Outdoor Activities and Adventure Sports
- ❖ Hiking, Trekking, and Mountain Climbing
- ❖ Lake Ohrid and Water Activities
- ❖ Winter Sports: Skiing and Snowboarding
- ❖ Nature Parks and Wildlife Exploration

Chapter 9: Culinary Experiences and Local Cuisine
- ❖ Introduction to Macedonian Cuisine
- ❖ Must-Try Dishes and Local Specialties
- ❖ Best Restaurants, Cafes, and Street Food
- ❖ Wineries, Distilleries, and Beverage Culture
- ❖ Food Markets and Traditional Cooking Classes

Chapter 10: Accommodation Options
- ❖ Luxury Hotels and Resorts
- ❖ Budget-Friendly Stays and Hostels
- ❖ Boutique Hotels and Traditional Guesthouses

- ❖ Tips for Booking and Contact Information

Chapter 11: Shopping and Souvenirs
- ❖ Local Markets and Artisan Shops
- ❖ Traditional Crafts and Products to Buy
- ❖ Popular Shopping Streets and Centers

Chapter 12: Culture, Festivals, and Local Etiquette
- ❖ Customs and Traditions
- ❖ Major Festivals and Events
- ❖ Art, Music, and Dance in Macedonian Culture
- ❖ Etiquette Tips for Travelers

Chapter 13: Practical Travel Tips and Final Essentials
- ❖ Emergency Numbers and Health Services
- ❖ Sustainable and Responsible Travel Advice
- ❖ Safety Tips for Travelers
- ❖ Useful Contacts: Tourist Centers, Embassies, and Consulates
- ❖ Conclusion

Chapter 1

Welcome to North Macedonia

History of North Macedonia: Lifestyle, Landscape, and Culture

1. History of North Macedonia

North Macedonia has a complex history shaped by various civilizations, including the ancient Macedonians, Romans, Byzantines, Ottomans, and Slavs. This diverse cultural heritage influences every aspect of its society, from architecture and traditions to language and cuisine.

- **Ancient Macedonia:** In the 4th century BCE, the kingdom of Macedon was ruled by Alexander the Great, who led one of history's most extensive empires. Though modern North Macedonia does not encompass the same territory, Alexander's legacy endures, particularly in the northern part of the country.

- **Roman and Byzantine Influence:** After the fall of ancient Macedonia, the region became a part of the Roman Empire and later the Byzantine Empire, leaving behind a legacy of Christian heritage, including early Christian churches and monasteries.

- **Ottoman Rule (1392–1912):** North Macedonia was under Ottoman rule for over five centuries. This period significantly influenced North Macedonian culture, particularly in architecture, cuisine, music, and religion, as evidenced by the mosques, Turkish baths, and Ottoman-style houses seen throughout the country.

- **Yugoslavian Period (1945–1991):** After World War II, North Macedonia was incorporated into socialist Yugoslavia, gaining greater autonomy as the Socialist Republic of Macedonia. This period marked significant modernization and the development of industry and infrastructure.

- **Modern Independence (1991–Present):** North Macedonia declared independence in 1991. However, the country faced issues around its name, which were resolved in 2019 when it officially became the Republic of North Macedonia. Today, it is a member of NATO and an EU candidate, progressively building a democratic, multicultural society.

2. Lifestyle and Culture of North Macedonia

The people of North Macedonia are known for their warmth, hospitality, and deep-rooted traditions. The lifestyle here blends old-world customs with contemporary influences, especially in urban areas like Skopje.

- **Hospitality:** Hospitality is deeply embedded in the Macedonian lifestyle. Guests are often welcomed with open arms, traditional foods, and the famous local brandy, "rakija." Macedonians view hosting visitors as a great honor and will go out of their way to make sure guests feel at home.

- **Family-Oriented Society:** Family plays a central role in Macedonian culture, and it's common for multiple generations to live under one roof. Social gatherings, family meals, and festivals are integral to Macedonian life, often bringing families together to celebrate and maintain cultural traditions.

- **Cultural Festivals:** Throughout the year, North Macedonia celebrates various festivals that showcase its music, dance, food, and religious traditions. The "Ohrid Summer Festival" and "Skopje Jazz Festival" are among the country's most prominent cultural events, drawing locals and tourists alike.

- **Traditional Music and Dance:** Macedonian folk music is unique, characterized by complex rhythms and traditional instruments like the "zurla" and "gajda" (bagpipes). "Oro" is a popular traditional dance, where people form a circle and perform intricate footwork, symbolizing unity and shared joy.

- **Cuisine:** Macedonian cuisine is hearty and diverse, with influences from Mediterranean, Turkish, and Slavic culinary traditions. Staples include "tavče gravče" (baked beans), "ajvar" (pepper spread), grilled meats, and various pastries. Fresh vegetables, local cheeses, and rich spices are commonly used, making Macedonian dishes vibrant and flavorful.

3. The Landscape of North Macedonia

North Macedonia is a scenic country, blessed with diverse landscapes that offer everything from rugged mountains to serene lakes.

- Mountains: Over 80% of North Macedonia is mountainous, with the Šar Mountains and the peaks of Mount Korab, Mount Pelister, and Galichica standing out. These areas are ideal for hiking, skiing, and mountaineering. The National Park of Mavrovo, the largest national park, is particularly famous for its dense forests, glacial lakes, and diverse wildlife.

- Lakes: North Macedonia is home to beautiful lakes, with Lake Ohrid being the most famous. This UNESCO World Heritage Site is one of Europe's oldest and deepest lakes, surrounded by mountains and dotted with monasteries, ancient churches, and traditional villages. Lake Prespa, shared with Albania and Greece, is another stunning body of water, known for its bird diversity and tranquil setting.

- Rivers and Valleys: The Vardar River, North Macedonia's longest river, flows from the northwest to the southeast, offering scenic river valleys and fertile plains. The Pelagonia Valley, for example, is an agricultural hub, with vineyards and orchards producing some of the best local wines.

- Thermal Springs: North Macedonia is known for its thermal springs, especially in Debar, Katlanovo, and Kumanovo. These mineral-rich waters are said to have healing properties and are popular for wellness tourism.

4. Religions and Cultural Heritage

North Macedonia is a culturally diverse country, with multiple ethnic groups and religions coexisting peacefully.

- **Religions:** The two major religions are Eastern Orthodoxy and Islam. The Orthodox Church is predominant among ethnic Macedonians, while a significant Albanian minority practices Islam. The country's religious tolerance is showcased in cities like Skopje and Tetovo, where churches and mosques stand side by side.

- **Architectural Heritage:** North Macedonia's architecture reflects its diverse history. In addition to ancient ruins and Ottoman-style houses, the capital, Skopje, has many modern buildings from the Yugoslav era. The "Skopje 2014" project added grandiose structures inspired by neoclassicism, giving the city a distinctive look.

- **UNESCO Sites:** The town of Ohrid, with its lake and numerous ancient churches, is North Macedonia's most famous UNESCO World Heritage site. It represents a living history, combining Byzantine, Roman, and Slavic heritage. Other notable heritage sites include the Painted Mosque in Tetovo and various Roman archaeological sites, like Stobi.

My Travel Experience To North Macedonia
Introduction to My Journey

North Macedonia was a revelation — a place where rich history, scenic landscapes, and cultural gems are woven into the daily life of its cities and towns. Each stop offered a blend of natural beauty and ancient heritage, with a warm local welcome at every turn. Here's a look at some must-visit spots that defined my experience in this remarkable Balkan country.

Skopje: The Captivating Capital
Skopje Fortress (Kale)

I started my exploration in Skopje, where the Skopje Fortress, or Kale, provided a glimpse into the city's long history and stunning views over the Vardar River and the vibrant cityscape. Walking along its ancient walls, I could feel the presence of centuries gone by. Built in the 6th century, the fortress has been a historical stronghold and is a perfect starting point for any North Macedonia journey.

- **Visitor Tips:** It's best to visit during the early morning or late afternoon for cooler temperatures and beautiful lighting over the city.
- **Getting There:** It's centrally located in Skopje, making it easy to reach on foot from most parts of the city.

Old Bazaar
The Old Bazaar was another highlight. This lively district is one of the largest and most well-preserved bazaars in the Balkans. Walking through its narrow alleys filled with local shops, tea houses, and mosques, I felt like I'd stepped back in time. The aroma of coffee, the artisans selling handmade crafts, and the call to prayer from nearby mosques all added to the experience.

- **Visitor Tips:** Try the local baklava or Turkish coffee at one of the traditional cafes and explore the shops for unique souvenirs, from handmade jewelry to antique books.

Lake Ohrid: The Jewel of North Macedonia
St. Naum Monastery
Lake Ohrid was magical. Nestled between mountain ranges,

its clear waters are home to several monasteries and ancient churches. The St. Naum Monastery, located on the southern shores, was a highlight of my visit to Lake Ohrid. Built in the 10th century, this Eastern Orthodox monastery is filled with frescoes and mosaics. I spent hours wandering the grounds and even took a peaceful boat ride to see the lake from a different perspective.

- Visitor Tips: It's common to take a day trip here, but if time allows, consider staying overnight in a nearby guesthouse to fully soak in the atmosphere.

Church of St. John at Kaneo
The Church of St. John at Kaneo sits on a cliff overlooking Lake Ohrid, and seeing it at sunset is breathtaking. The peaceful setting, combined with the centuries-old architecture and the panoramic views of the lake, made this an unforgettable experience. This church, with its intricate brickwork and dramatic location, is an iconic North Macedonian image.

- Visitor Tips: Try to arrive an hour before sunset to find a good viewing spot — it's a popular time to visit, and the views are worth the wait.

Bitola: A Walk Through Ancient Ruins and Vibrant Streets
Heraclea Lyncestis
In Bitola, I explored Heraclea Lyncestis, an ancient Macedonian city founded by Philip II, father of Alexander the

Great. The site features mosaics, a theater, and remains of early Christian basilicas, each layer adding to the story of this city. Wandering among these ruins was like stepping back into antiquity, with incredible mosaics still vibrant after centuries.

- **Visitor Tips:** Local guides are available and provide excellent insights into the history of the site. Comfortable shoes are a must, as the terrain can be uneven.

Širok Sokak Street
Bitola's Širok Sokak is a pedestrian boulevard lined with cafes, shops, and neoclassical architecture. This street was full of life, and it was the perfect place to enjoy local Macedonian cuisine or to simply relax and watch the world go by. I recommend trying a "tavče gravče" (baked beans) dish with a local rakija.

- **Visitor Tips:** The street is particularly lively in the evenings when locals come out for a "korzo" (stroll) with friends and family.

Mavrovo National Park: North Macedonia's Natural Wonderland
Hiking and Scenic Drives
To experience North Macedonia's natural side, Mavrovo National Park was a perfect choice. The park's vast landscapes include the stunning Mavrovo Lake and rolling mountain ranges that are ideal for hiking. I took a scenic drive through the park and spent a day hiking near Lake Mavrovo. The fresh mountain air, serene lake views, and encounters

with local shepherds made this an exceptional outdoor experience.

- Visitor Tips: Some trails are well-marked, but for longer hikes, consider hiring a local guide. There are also great picnic spots around the lake, perfect for a packed lunch.

St. Jovan Bigorski Monastery
Nestled within the Mavrovo mountains, St. Jovan Bigorski Monastery is a serene place of worship, known for its intricate woodwork and serene surroundings. It was a peaceful end to my trip through the park, with a sense of calmness and spirituality that was truly moving.

- Visitor Tips: Make sure to dress respectfully, as this is an active place of worship. The monastery shop has some unique handcrafted souvenirs that support the local community.

From the lively streets of Skopje to the serene shores of Lake Ohrid and the dramatic landscapes of Mavrovo, North Macedonia is a country of contrasts and beauty. Its historical sites, natural parks, and vibrant cities each left a lasting impression. This journey introduced me to a warm and welcoming culture, and each visit offered a deeper understanding of the country's heritage and landscapes. I left North Macedonia with unforgettable memories and a desire to return and explore even more.

Key Highlights and Unique Features of North Macedonia

1. Cultural Crossroads of East and West
North Macedonia's location has long placed it at the crossroads of different civilizations, including the Romans, Byzantines, Ottomans, and Slavs. This cultural melting pot is evident in the architecture, art, cuisine, and languages spoken throughout the country. From Orthodox monasteries and Ottoman mosques to modern art galleries and theaters, the cultural diversity here is remarkable.

2. Majestic Natural Landscapes
The country is known for its picturesque mountains, deep lakes, and scenic valleys. Notable sites like Lake Ohrid, one of the oldest and deepest lakes in Europe, and Mavrovo National Park, with its rich biodiversity and scenic trails, make North Macedonia a haven for nature lovers. Its national parks, waterfalls, and rugged mountain ranges are ideal for

outdoor activities, including hiking, skiing, and mountain biking.

3. Historic Cities and Ancient Sites
The ancient city of Ohrid is a UNESCO World Heritage Site, often called the "Jerusalem of the Balkans" due to its multitude of churches and monasteries. Bitola, Skopje, and Stobi also boast significant historical attractions, such as Roman ruins, Ottoman bazaars, and historic monuments, all providing a window into North Macedonia's past. The Skopje Fortress, the Old Bazaar in Skopje, and the Heraclea Lyncestis ruins in Bitola are must-visit spots.

4. Rich Culinary Scene
North Macedonian cuisine is an enticing blend of Balkan, Mediterranean, and Turkish influences. Dishes like "ajvar" (red pepper spread), "tavče gravče" (baked beans), and "shopska salad" showcase local ingredients and flavors. The country is also known for its wine production, especially around the Tikveš wine region. A local meal, often shared with friends and family, is accompanied by rakija, a strong fruit brandy popular in the region.

5. Affordable Travel Destination
North Macedonia remains a budget-friendly travel destination compared to other European countries. Accommodations, dining, and activities tend to be reasonably priced, making it ideal for travelers seeking a high-value experience. Public transport is also inexpensive, and local markets offer affordable and delicious street food.

Top Reasons to Visit North Macedonia

1. Experience Lake Ohrid's Serenity and Historic Charm

Lake Ohrid, a UNESCO World Heritage Site, is renowned for its crystal-clear waters and scenic beauty. The lake is also home to charming villages, historic churches, and the iconic Church of St. John at Kaneo, set on a cliff overlooking the lake. Lake Ohrid is perfect for relaxing, boating, and exploring centuries-old sites. It's especially stunning at sunset, when the lake and the surrounding mountains take on a golden hue.

2. Discover Skopje's Fusion of Modern and Ancient

Skopje, the capital city, offers a mix of modern architecture, historical sites, and a lively urban scene. The city's attractions include the massive "Warrior on a Horse" statue, the Kale Fortress, and the Stone Bridge, which connects the old and new parts of the city. Visitors can also explore the Old Bazaar, filled with traditional shops, cafes, and historical mosques, or visit the Mother Teresa Memorial House, honoring one of Skopje's most famous figures.

3. Dive into Macedonian History in Bitola
Bitola, known as the "city of consuls," has a rich Ottoman-era history and a vibrant cultural scene. Širok Sokak, its main pedestrian street, is lined with cafes and shops housed in neoclassical buildings. A visit to Heraclea Lyncestis, an ancient city with impressive Roman ruins, gives insight into the area's historical significance. Bitola's relaxed atmosphere and welcoming locals make it an ideal spot for enjoying local life.

4. Hike Through Stunning National Parks
North Macedonia is home to several breathtaking national parks, including Mavrovo, Pelister, and Galichica. Mavrovo National Park is ideal for hiking, skiing, and spotting wildlife like the Balkan lynx. Pelister National Park offers beautiful alpine scenery and a unique biodiversity, including the rare Molika pine tree. These parks cater to nature lovers and adventure seekers alike, offering trails for all skill levels.

5. Taste Local Wine and Cuisine
The Tikveš region, known as North Macedonia's "wine country," is one of the oldest wine-producing regions in Europe. It's home to several wineries where visitors can enjoy tastings and tours. Macedonian wines, such as Vranec (a red wine) and Smederevka (a white wine), pair well with local dishes like grilled meats, roasted vegetables, and pastries.

Food lovers will also enjoy exploring Macedonian markets, where they can try fresh cheeses, bread, and seasonal produce.

Making Friends in North Macedonia

1. Embrace the Warm Hospitality
North Macedonians are known for their warm hospitality and are often eager to share their culture with visitors. Many locals are happy to introduce travelers to their traditions, cuisine, and customs. In smaller towns and rural areas, it's not uncommon to be invited for coffee or a meal, especially if you show genuine interest in their culture.

2. Learn a Few Local Words and Phrases
Speaking even a few basic words of Macedonian, such as "dobar den" (hello) or "blagodaram" (thank you), can go a long way in breaking the ice. North Macedonians appreciate when travelers make an effort to learn their language, even if it's just a few words. English is commonly spoken in larger

cities, but a little local language can create a friendly connection.

3. Join Local Festivities and Events
Throughout the year, North Macedonia celebrates various festivals and events that provide great opportunities to meet locals. The Ohrid Summer Festival, a renowned event featuring music, theater, and dance, is one of the biggest in the country. Attending these festivals, often held in public squares and historic venues, allows you to join in the communal spirit and connect with the community.

4. Experience the Cafe Culture
In cities like Skopje, Ohrid, and Bitola, locals enjoy spending time in cafes with friends and family. Joining this laid-back cafe culture is a great way to meet locals and experience daily life. Order a Turkish coffee or Macedonian tea and strike up a conversation — many North Macedonians are friendly and open to chatting with visitors.

5. Participate in Outdoor Activities
Outdoor activities, such as hiking, skiing, and cycling, are popular pastimes in North Macedonia. Joining guided hikes or skiing in Mavrovo National Park, for example, is an excellent way to meet locals who share a love for nature and outdoor adventure. Many local adventure companies and guides are happy to share their knowledge of the country's landscapes and wildlife.

6. Respect Local Customs and Traditions

Showing respect for North Macedonian customs is essential in building positive relationships. When visiting religious sites, dress modestly and follow any guidelines for visitors. In social settings, showing appreciation for food and drinks offered to you is a sign of respect, as hospitality is highly valued. A warm smile and politeness can go a long way toward forming connections with locals.

Chapter 2

Planning Your Trip To North Macedonia

Entry and Visa Requirements

1. Visa Policy Overview
North Macedonia's visa policy is generally traveler-friendly. Citizens of the European Union, the United States, Canada, the UK, Australia, New Zealand, and several other countries can enter North Macedonia visa-free for up to 90 days within a 180-day period. For travelers from countries that require a visa, it's best to apply through a North Macedonian embassy or consulate in your home country before traveling.

2. Passport Requirements
Your passport must be valid for at least six months beyond your planned departure date from North Macedonia. It's important to check the passport validity requirements well in advance to avoid any last-minute issues at border control.

3. Extension of Stay
If you wish to extend your stay beyond the 90-day period, you can apply for an extension at the Ministry of Internal Affairs in North Macedonia. Extensions are granted on a case-by-case basis, so make sure to provide a valid reason and sufficient documentation.

4. Registration Requirement
Foreign visitors staying longer than 24 hours are required to register with the police. If you're staying at a hotel, hostel, or Airbnb, they will typically handle this process for you. However, if you're staying in a private residence, you'll need to visit a local police station within 24 hours of arrival.

5. Schengen Visa Holders
While North Macedonia is not a Schengen Area country, it allows Schengen visa holders to enter and stay for up to 15 days, provided they meet other entry requirements.

Customs Rules and Regulations
1. Currency and Cash Declaration
Travelers entering North Macedonia must declare any cash amounts exceeding €10,000. It's advisable to carry a combination of cash and a credit or debit card, as card

payments may not be widely accepted in rural areas. The local currency is the Macedonian Denar (MKD), and it's recommended to exchange currency at official exchange offices or banks to avoid high fees.

2. Restricted and Prohibited Items

North Macedonia restricts the import of certain items, including firearms, explosives, narcotics, and certain animal and plant products. Additionally, cultural artifacts and antiques are subject to strict regulations and cannot be exported without proper documentation. Avoid bringing items such as fruits, vegetables, and raw meat, as these may be confiscated at customs.

3. Duty-Free Allowances

Travelers are allowed to bring duty-free items into North Macedonia within the following limits:

- **Alcohol:** Up to 1 liter of spirits, 2 liters of wine, or 5 liters of beer.
- **Tobacco:** Up to 200 cigarettes, 100 cigarillos, 50 cigars, or 250g of tobacco.
- **Perfume and Gifts:** Small quantities for personal use only.

4. Photography and Drone Regulations

Certain areas, especially military or government buildings, may prohibit photography. Additionally, if you plan to use a drone, you may need to obtain permission from the Civil Aviation Agency, as regulations apply for drone usage in North Macedonia.

Health, Safety, and Travel Insurance

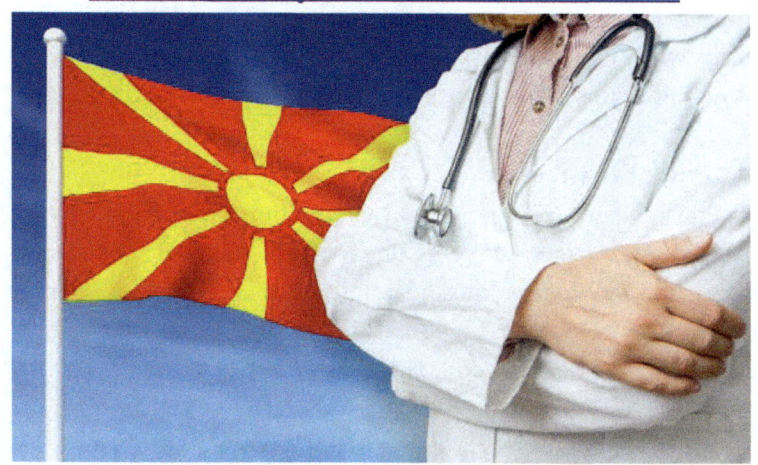

1. Recommended Vaccinations
While no vaccinations are required for entry, it's recommended to ensure you're up-to-date on routine vaccines such as MMR, tetanus, and hepatitis A. If you plan to travel in rural areas or engage in outdoor activities, you might consider vaccinations for hepatitis B and rabies.

2. Health and Medical Services
North Macedonia offers quality healthcare services, especially in major cities like Skopje and Bitola. However, healthcare facilities in remote areas may be limited. Carry a small first-aid kit with essentials, as pharmacies may not always stock international brands.

3. Safety Precautions

North Macedonia is generally safe for travelers, with low crime rates in most areas. Petty theft can occur in crowded tourist spots or markets, so keep your belongings secure. It's also wise to avoid discussing sensitive political topics, as regional issues can sometimes lead to misunderstandings.

4. Travel Insurance
Travel insurance is highly recommended for North Macedonia, as it covers unexpected medical costs, trip cancellations, lost belongings, and other emergencies. Ensure your policy includes medical evacuation, as some remote areas may lack advanced healthcare facilities.

Best Times to Visit and Seasonal Tips
1. Spring (April to June)
Spring is one of the best times to visit, with mild temperatures and blooming landscapes. This season is ideal for outdoor activities like hiking in Mavrovo or Pelister National Park and exploring the historical sites in cities such as Ohrid and Skopje.

2. Summer (July to September)
Summer in North Macedonia is warm, particularly in July and August when temperatures can reach 30°C (86°F) or higher. This is peak tourist season around Lake Ohrid, where visitors enjoy water activities and local festivals. It's wise to book accommodations in advance if traveling in summer and to bring sun protection for the warmer days.

3. Autumn (September to November)

Autumn is a fantastic season for both weather and scenery, with fewer tourists and a comfortable climate. The vineyards in the Tikveš region come alive with harvest activities, making it an excellent time to sample North Macedonian wines.

4. Winter (December to March)
Winter can be cold, especially in mountainous areas where temperatures often dip below freezing. Ski resorts in Mavrovo attract winter sports enthusiasts, and the festive atmosphere around the New Year can be enjoyable in cities. Be prepared for colder temperatures and potentially snowy conditions in higher altitudes.

Suggested Packing List

General Packing Tips
1. Clothing:

- **Layering:** The weather can vary, so pack layers. Consider lightweight t-shirts, long-sleeve shirts, and a warm sweater or jacket.
   - **Comfortable Footwear:** Bring sturdy walking shoes for exploring cities and hiking boots if you plan to hike.
   - **Dress Modestly:** In rural areas and places of worship, it's respectful to dress modestly. Women should have skirts or dresses that cover the knees, and men should avoid shorts in such areas.
   - **Weather-Specific Gear:** Depending on the season, pack accordingly (e.g., a rain jacket for the rainy season, warm clothing for winter, and breathable fabrics for summer).

2. Accessories:
   - **Sun Protection:** Sunglasses, a wide-brimmed hat, and sunscreen are essential, especially in summer.
   - **Travel Umbrella:** Useful for unexpected rain showers.
   - **Reusable Water Bottle:** Stay hydrated while reducing plastic waste.

3. Toiletries:
   - Bring travel-sized toiletries and any specific products you prefer, as availability may vary.
   - Don't forget personal medications and a basic first-aid kit.

4. Electronics:
   - **Universal Adapter:** North Macedonia uses the Europlug (Type C) and Schuko (Type E/F) sockets, so bring a suitable adapter.
   - **Power Bank:** Useful for keeping devices charged while on the go.

5. Travel Documents:
   - Carry copies of your passport, travel insurance, and any necessary visas.
   - Keep a digital backup of important documents.

Men-Specific Packing Tips
- **Smart Casual Wear:** Pack a few smart casual outfits for dining or events.
- **Swimwear:** If you plan to visit lakes or pools, include swim trunks.
- **Belts and Accessories:** Consider bringing belts and minimal accessories to enhance outfits.

Women-Specific Packing Tips
- **Versatile Dresses:** Dresses that can be dressed up or down are ideal for various occasions.
- **Scarves or Shawls:** Useful for covering shoulders in religious sites or as an accessory.
- **Makeup and Accessories:** Pack light but include essentials for a polished look.

Additional Tips
- **Daypack:** A small backpack for day trips can be handy for carrying essentials.
- Snacks: Consider packing some energy bars or snacks for day trips or hikes.
- **Laundry Bag:** A small bag for dirty clothes can help keep your suitcase organized.

- **First Aid Kit:** Basic supplies, including any prescription medications, pain relievers, and antiseptic wipes.
- **Personal Care Items:** Toilet paper and hand sanitizer can be useful, especially in remote areas.
- **Umbrella or Rain Jacket:** Useful during unexpected rain showers, especially in spring and autumn.
- **Map or Offline GPS:** Reliable internet may not be available in rural areas, so an offline GPS app can be helpful.

Budgeting Tips

1. Accommodation
- **Types of Lodging:** North Macedonia offers a range of accommodation options, from budget hostels and guesthouses to mid-range hotels and luxury resorts.
- **Estimated Costs:**
  - **Hostels:** €10-€20 per night for a dormitory bed.
  - **Guesthouses:** €20-€40 per night for a private room.
  - **Hotels:** €40-€100 per night for mid-range hotels.
- **Booking Tips:** Use platforms like Booking.com or Airbnb to compare prices and book in advance for better deals, especially in peak tourist seasons.

2. Transportation
- **Public Transport:** Buses are the primary mode of transport within cities and between towns.
  - **Local Buses:** Tickets cost around €0.50-€1 per ride.
  - Intercity Buses: Fares vary by distance, typically ranging from €5-€20.
- **Taxis:** Starting fare is about €0.50, with additional costs per kilometer (approximately €0.50-€0.70).

- **Car Rentals:** Renting a car can range from €30-€60 per day. Fuel prices are about €1.30 per liter.
- **Tip:** Use apps like Bolt for affordable ride-hailing services in urban areas.

3. Food and Dining
- **Eating Out:** North Macedonia is known for its affordable dining options.
  - **Street Food:** Try local snacks like burek (savory pastry) or kebabs for about €2-€5.
  - **Casual Restaurants:** Meals range from €5-€15, depending on the dish and location.
  - **Mid-Range Restaurants:** Expect to pay €15-€30 for a three-course meal.
- **Self-Catering:** Shopping at local markets (like Bitola's market) or supermarkets (such as Skopje City Mall) can help you save money on meals, with costs around €20-€30 for groceries per week.

4. Activities and Attractions
- **Entry Fees:** Many museums and cultural sites charge reasonable entrance fees (approximately €2-€5).
- **Free Activities:** Enjoy hiking in national parks (like Mavrovo or Pelister), exploring the beautiful Lake Ohrid, and visiting historical sites without an entry fee.
- **Guided Tours:** If you prefer organized activities, expect to pay around €20-€50 for day tours or excursions.

5. Currency and Payment Methods

- **Currency:** The official currency is the Macedonian Denar (MKD). As of now, €1 is approximately MKD 61.
- **ATMs and Credit Cards:** ATMs are widely available in cities. Credit cards are accepted in most establishments, but it's wise to carry cash for smaller vendors and rural areas.
- **Budgeting Tip:** Monitor your spending using budgeting apps to keep track of expenses.

6. Seasonal Considerations
- **Travel Off-Peak:** Consider visiting during the shoulder seasons (April-June, September-October) to benefit from lower prices on accommodation and fewer crowds.
- **Festivals and Events:** Check local calendars for festivals that may have entrance fees or special costs associated with events.

7. Travel Insurance
- **Importance:** Invest in travel insurance to protect against unexpected costs like medical emergencies or trip cancellations.
- **Estimated Cost:** Basic coverage can range from €20-€50 for a week, depending on the policy.

8. Sample Daily Budget
- **Budget Traveler:** €30-€50 per day (hostel, street food, public transport).
- **Mid-Range Traveler:** €70-€120 per day (guesthouse, casual dining, car rental).
- **Luxury Traveler:** €150+ per day (hotel, fine dining, private tours).

Final Tips

- **Local Insights:** Ask locals for recommendations on affordable eateries and hidden gems to enhance your experience without overspending.

- **Travel Apps:** Download apps for maps, transportation, and translation to ease navigation and communication while minimizing costs.

By planning and budgeting wisely, you can enjoy a fulfilling and enriching experience in North Macedonia without breaking the bank.

Chapter 3

Getting to North Macedonia

Major Airports and Airlines

1. Skopje International Airport (SKP)
  - **Location:** About 17 km east of Skopje, the capital city.
  - **Overview:** This is the primary international gateway to North Macedonia and handles the majority of international flights. It features modern facilities and services, including duty-free shops, restaurants, and car rental services.
  - **Airlines Operating:**
    - **Low-cost Airlines:** Wizz Air, Ryanair, easyJet
    - **Traditional Airlines:** Turkish Airlines, Lufthansa, Air Serbia

- **Destinations:** Popular routes include flights to major European cities such as Vienna, London, Belgrade, and Frankfurt.

2. Ohrid Airport (OHD)
- **Location:** Approximately 10 km from the town of Ohrid, a UNESCO World Heritage site.
- **Overview:** This airport serves mainly seasonal flights catering to tourists visiting Lake Ohrid.
- Airlines Operating:
    - **Seasonal Carriers:** Wizz Air, easyJet, and charter airlines during peak summer months.
- **Destinations:** Commonly serviced routes include flights to cities like Basel, London, and various Balkan cities.

Tips for Border Crossings
1. Documents Required:
- **Passport:** Ensure your passport is valid for at least six months beyond your date of entry.
- **Visa:** Check if you need a visa to enter North Macedonia. Citizens of EU countries, the U.S., Canada, and several others can enter visa-free for short stays.

2. Customs Regulations:
- **Duty-Free Allowances:** Familiarize yourself with what you can bring into the country duty-free (e.g., alcohol, tobacco).
- **Prohibited Items:** Avoid bringing in items like drugs, weapons, and certain agricultural products.

3. Border Crossing Procedures:
   - **Use Official Checkpoints:** Only cross borders at designated points to avoid fines or legal issues.
   - Wait Times: Be prepared for potential waiting times at busy crossings, especially during peak travel seasons.

4. Transportation Options:
   - **Public Transport:** Buses are available at major border crossings, making it easy to reach cities like Skopje or Ohrid.
   - **Car Rentals:** If driving from neighboring countries, ensure you have appropriate insurance and vehicle documentation.

Overview of Flights and Common Layovers

1. Flight Options:
   - **Direct Flights:** There are direct flights to North Macedonia from various European cities, mainly through Skopje International Airport.
   - **Connecting Flights:** For travelers from regions outside Europe, connections are typically made in cities like Vienna, Belgrade, Istanbul, or Zurich.

2. Common Layover Cities:
   - **Vienna (VIE):** A major hub for connecting flights to North Macedonia, with numerous daily connections.
   - **Istanbul (IST):** Turkish Airlines offers several flights to Skopje from Istanbul, making it a popular layover city for long-haul travelers.

- **Belgrade (BEG):** The proximity to Skopje makes Belgrade a frequent stop for many flights.
- **Zagreb (ZAG):** Some travelers may find layovers here, especially those flying from Western Europe or connecting from Croatia.

3. Travel Time Considerations:
- **From Major European Cities:** Flights from London to Skopje typically take about 3 hours, while flights from Frankfurt or Amsterdam are around 2-2.5 hours.
- **Long-Haul Connections:** For travelers flying from North America, expect total travel times (including layovers) to be 12 hours or more, depending on your connection.

Additional Tips

- **Booking Flights:** Use flight comparison websites to find the best deals. Booking in advance, especially during the summer tourist season, is advisable.
- **Local Transportation:** Upon arrival, familiarize yourself with local transportation options, including taxis, shuttles, and public buses, to navigate to your accommodation.
- **Language Considerations:** While many people in urban areas speak English, learning a few basic phrases in Macedonian can be helpful and appreciated by locals.

Chapter 4

Essential Travel Information

Currency and Exchange, Banks, and ATMs

Currency
North Macedonia's official currency is the Macedonian Denar (MKD), symbolized as ден or MKD. You'll find banknotes in denominations of 10, 50, 100, 500, 1000, and 5000 MKD, while coins come in smaller values like 1, 2, 5, 10, and 50 denars.

Exchange Tips
Currency exchange is easy at banks, licensed exchange offices, and sometimes hotels, but exchange offices and banks in Skopje and other large cities often have the best rates.

Avoid airport exchanges if possible, as they generally offer less favorable rates. Euros, US dollars, and British pounds are the most accepted foreign currencies. While credit cards are widely used in urban centers, it's a good idea to carry some cash, particularly if you plan to explore rural areas where cash is more common.

Banks and ATMs

North Macedonia's major banks include Komercijalna Banka, Stopanska Banka, and NLB Banka, with banking hours typically from 8:30 AM to 4:30 PM, Monday to Friday, and some open until noon on Saturdays. ATMs are easily accessible in cities and popular tourist areas and support most international cards like Visa and MasterCard. Be aware that a small withdrawal fee may apply at some ATMs, so it's helpful to confirm any international ATM fees with your home bank. If entering or leaving the country with more than 10,000 euros in cash, you'll need to declare it to customs.

To banks to open North Macedonia

1. Komercijalna Banka AD Skopje

   - **Address:** Orce Nikolov St. 3, 1000 Skopje, North Macedonia

   - **Website:** https://www.kb.com.mk

   - Services: Komercijalna Banka is one of the largest and oldest banks in North Macedonia, offering a wide range of services including personal and business accounts, loans, savings, investments, and online banking.

   - **Documents Needed for Account Opening:**

- Passport or valid North Macedonian ID (for residents).
- Proof of address (e.g., utility bill, rental contract).
- Employment verification or source of funds for certain accounts.
- **For businesses:** Registration certificate, tax identification, and proof of company ownership.
- **Online Banking Services:** Komercijalna Banka offers secure online banking through its web portal and mobile application, allowing for transfers, bill payments, account management, and more.

2. NLB Banka AD Skopje

- **Address:** Mother Teresa 1, 1000 Skopje, North Macedonia
- **Website:** https://www.nlb.mk
- **Services:** NLB Banka provides personal and business banking services, including credit cards, personal loans, mortgages, and financial advising. It also features robust online banking and mobile app options.
- Documents Needed for Account Opening:
  - Valid ID or passport.
  - Proof of residence.
  - Employment documentation or proof of income for certain accounts.
- **For companies:** Business registration, proof of ownership, and tax identification.
- **Online Banking Services:** Through the NLB Klik platform, users can handle transactions, payments, and investment management. The NLB Pay app also facilitates easy mobile payments and contactless transactions.

3. Stopanska Banka AD Skopje

- **Address:** 11 Oktomvri Blvd. No.7, 1000 Skopje, North Macedonia
- **Website:**
https://www.stb.com.mk
- **Services:** Offering a variety of services from everyday banking to investment products, Stopanska Banka is particularly known for its customer-focused personal and corporate banking services.
- Documents Needed for Account Opening:
  - Valid North Macedonian ID or passport.
  - Address proof such as a recent utility bill or lease agreement.
  - Employment or income proof for specific account types.
- **For businesses:** Company registration, tax number, and proof of company representation.
- **Online Banking Services:** The e-banking platform from Stopanska Banka allows users to transfer funds, pay bills, view account history, and more. Mobile banking is also available for convenient access on the go.

4. Halkbank AD Skopje
- **Address:** Sveti Kiril i Metodij St. 54, 1000 Skopje, North Macedonia
- **Website:**
https://www.halkbank.mk
- Services: Halkbank provides a range of financial services, including personal and corporate banking, loans, credit cards, and investment products. It also offers competitive savings accounts and flexible credit options.
- Documents Needed for Account Opening:
  - Passport or North Macedonian ID.

- Proof of residence.
   - Income verification (for credit accounts or loans).
   - Business accounts require registration documents and tax information.
   - Online Banking Services: Halkbank's internet banking platform and mobile app offer full account management, bill payments, and loan tracking services.

5. ProCredit Bank Macedonia
   - Address: Aleksandar Makedonski Blvd. 12, 1000 Skopje, North Macedonia
   - Website: https://www.pcb.mk
   - Services: ProCredit Bank specializes in providing services for small to medium-sized businesses and individual banking needs. They focus on transparent banking practices and offer savings, credit, and investment options.
   - Documents Needed for Account Opening:
   - Valid ID or passport.
   - Proof of address.
   - Income or employment details, depending on the account type.
   - For business accounts, registration certificates, proof of ownership, and tax information.
   - Online Banking Services: ProCredit offers a secure online banking platform, featuring remote account management, online payments, and easy access to banking records.

Online-Only Banks in North Macedonia
Online-only banking options in North Macedonia include some international banks that allow account openings through online platforms and serve international clients. Although they

do not have physical branches, these banks often offer currency flexibility, ease of access, and minimal fees. Some popular choices include:

1. Revolut
 - **Website:**
https://www.revolut.com
   - **Services:** Offers multi-currency accounts, international transfers, budgeting tools, and currency exchange. Revolut is popular for its low fees on international transactions.
   - **Account Requirements:**
     - Valid passport or ID.
     - Proof of address (usually verified digitally).
     - Mobile phone for two-factor authentication.

2. N26
   - **Website:** https://www.n26.com
   - **Services:** N26 provides international banking with features like multi-currency accounts, budgeting tools, and no foreign transaction fees.
   - **Account Requirements:**
     - Passport or ID.
     - Address verification (usually digital).
     - A smartphone with the N26 app.

3. Wise (formerly TransferWise)
   - **Website:** https://wise.com
   - **Services:** Wise is best for low-cost international money transfers and offers multi-currency accounts with borderless features.
   - **Account Requirements:**

- Valid ID and address proof (may vary based on location).
- A linked bank account for transfers.

Language Basics and Key Phrases
Official Language
The official language in North Macedonia is Macedonian, which uses the Cyrillic alphabet. In certain areas, particularly the western and northern parts, Albanian is also commonly spoken. Although English is generally understood in urban areas and among younger people, learning a few basic phrases in Macedonian will be helpful.

Key Macedonian Phrases
Here are some essential phrases to assist you during your travels:

- **Hello:** "Zdravo"
- **Goodbye:** "Doviduvanje"
- **Please:** "Ve molam"
- **Thank you:** "Blagodaram"
- **Yes:** "Da"
- **No:** "Ne"
- **How much is this?:** "Kolku chini?"
- **I don't understand:** "Ne razbiram"
- **Do you speak English?:** "Zboruvate li angliski?"

Using these basic greetings and questions can make your interactions smoother and show locals that you're making an effort.

Local Laws and Customs

Cultural Etiquette

North Macedonia has a rich cultural blend of Christian Orthodox and Muslim traditions, so it's respectful to be aware of both. When visiting religious sites, dress modestly, as women might need to cover their heads, and everyone should cover their shoulders and knees. Handshakes are a common greeting, but close friends or family may greet each other with a kiss on each cheek. When invited into someone's home, bringing a small gift like flowers or sweets is considered thoughtful.

Legal Aspects

Always carry a copy of your passport, as you might need it for identification at hotels, police checks, or even certain purchases. Public intoxication and loud or disruptive behavior are generally frowned upon, and it's prohibited to consume alcohol in some public areas. When it comes to photography, be cautious about photographing people without permission, especially in rural areas, and avoid taking photos of military or government buildings.

Smoking Restrictions

Smoking is common in North Macedonia but is restricted in certain indoor spaces, like malls, hospitals, and government buildings. Keep an eye out for designated smoking areas to avoid any issues.

Travel Safety

North Macedonia is considered safe for travelers, but, as with any destination, it's wise to keep an eye on your belongings and use general travel precautions, especially in crowded spots where pickpocketing can occur.

Connectivity: SIM Cards, Wi-Fi, and Internet Tips

SIM Cards

For mobile connectivity, North Macedonia's main telecom providers are Makedonski Telekom, A1 Macedonia, and Lycamobile. You can purchase SIM cards at the airport, retail stores, or the provider's shops, with packages that typically include data, local calls, and texts. These starter SIM packages are budget-friendly, costing around 300-500 MKD (about 5-8 USD). You'll need your passport to register and activate the SIM card, which is usually quick and hassle-free.

Wi-Fi Access

Wi-Fi is widely available in hotels, hostels, and guesthouses across cities and tourist hubs like Skopje, Bitola, and Ohrid. Many cafes and restaurants also provide free Wi-Fi, and some public squares and tourist sites offer it as well. However, exercise caution with public networks, especially for sensitive transactions. If you plan to stay longer or visit remote areas, buying a portable Wi-Fi device or relying on a robust mobile data package is advisable.

Internet Tips

Opt for tourist-specific data packages from Makedonski Telekom or A1 for seamless connectivity, which are sufficient for basic browsing, GPS, and social media use. Since connectivity in remote areas might be unreliable, it's wise to download offline maps on your device to ensure you can navigate even without internet access.

Chapter 5

Getting Around North Macedonia

Public Transportation in North Macedonia

Buses
 - **Overview:** Buses are the primary mode of public transport across North Macedonia, especially in cities like Skopje, Bitola, and Ohrid. The bus system is generally reliable and budget-friendly, with routes connecting major towns and tourist areas.
 - **Tickets & Payment:** Tickets can be bought at bus terminals, on the bus (in some cases), or through electronic payment cards in Skopje. The Skopje City Card is a

rechargeable card that offers convenience for regular bus users within the city.
- **Major Bus Operators:**
- **Manora Bus:** Operates long-distance routes within North Macedonia and nearby countries.
- **Galeb Ohrid:** Services routes in the Ohrid area and long-distance connections.
- **Address for Skopje Central Bus Station:** Bul. Kuzman Josifovski Pitu No. 17, Skopje, North Macedonia.

Trains
- **Overview:** North Macedonia has a limited but scenic railway network operated by Makedonski Zeleznici Transport (Macedonian Railways), primarily connecting Skopje with towns like Bitola, Prilep, and Gevgelija.
- **Tickets & Payment:** Train tickets are affordable and can be purchased at stations or on the train. Prices are generally lower than buses, though trains are often slower.
- **Main Train Routes:**
- **Skopje to Bitola:** A picturesque journey passing through the Vardar Valley.
- **Skopje to Thessaloniki (Greece):** International route available in summer, subject to schedule.

Taxis
- **Overview:** Taxis are widely available in cities and towns. They are affordable by European standards, but it's advised to use licensed taxis with meters to avoid overcharging.
- **Fares & Tips:** Expect rates around 0.50 to 1 EUR per kilometer in Skopje. Confirm the rate before starting the journey if the taxi lacks a meter.

- **Popular Taxi Companies in Skopje:**
  - **City Taxi Skopje:** +389 2 15 133
  - **Taxi Narodna:** +389 2 15 177

Car Rentals and Driving Tips

Top Car Rental Companies
 - **Europcar North Macedonia**
   - **Address:** Skopje International Airport, Petrovec, 1043 Skopje
   - **Location:** Available at the airport and central Skopje, making it convenient for tourists.
 - **Hertz North Macedonia**
   - **Address:** Skopje International Airport and multiple urban locations.
   - **Location:** Offers a large fleet of vehicles, from economy to luxury.
 - Sixt Rent a Car
   - **Address:** Blvd. Kuzman Josifovski Pitu 15, 1000 Skopje, North Macedonia

- **Location:** Known for its online booking platform and convenient pick-up/drop-off points across the country.

Driving Tips
- **License & Documentation:** An international driver's license is recommended, especially for non-EU citizens. Carry your passport, rental documents, and insurance at all times.
- **Road Conditions & Traffic:** Major highways are in good condition, though rural roads may have rough patches. Traffic can be heavy in cities but is manageable.
- **Speed Limits:** Generally, 50 km/h in cities, 80 km/h on open roads, and 120 km/h on highways. Fines are enforced for speeding.
- **Parking:** Street parking is available in cities, with some metered spaces. Parking garages and lots can be found in Skopje. Always check signs for permitted parking zones.

Biking, Walking Tours, and Eco-Friendly Travel Options

- **Biking:** Biking is increasingly popular, especially in cities like Skopje, where bike-sharing programs and rental shops are available.
- **Nextbike Skopje:** A bike-sharing system with multiple stations across Skopje. Simply register through the app, find a bike station, and start exploring.
- **Walking Tours:** Many cities offer walking tours, including historical and cultural tours in Skopje and Ohrid. These tours are eco-friendly and provide a more immersive experience.
- Popular Walking Tours:

- **Skopje Walking Tour:** Covers main attractions like the Stone Bridge, Macedonia Square, and the Old Bazaar.
- **Ohrid Historical Tour:** A UNESCO World Heritage walk through Ohrid, covering churches, monasteries, and the old town.
- **Eco-Friendly Travel Tips:**
- Use public transportation, bike rentals, or walk to minimize environmental impact.
- Avoid plastic by carrying reusable water bottles and bags. Tap water is safe to drink in North Macedonia.
- Choose eco-conscious accommodations, some of which may have energy-efficient practices or sustainable tourism certifications.

Travel Apps and Helpful Resources

- **Skopje City Card App:** Enables users to purchase and recharge Skopje City Cards for bus travel. Offers route information, schedules, and fare details.
- **Nextbike App:** Essential for accessing Skopje's bike-sharing service. You can locate bike stations, check bike availability, and pay for rentals directly through the app.
- **Moovit:** A navigation app that helps with public transportation routes, schedules, and nearby stops. Works for buses and trains across North Macedonia.
- **Google Maps:** Helpful for navigating North Macedonia's cities and countryside. Download offline maps before traveling, especially for rural areas with limited internet access.
- **Booking.com and Airbnb:** Essential for finding accommodation options from hotels to apartments.

Booking.com often includes eco-friendly filters for sustainable stays.

- **iTaxi:** Allows you to book taxis in Skopje and other cities, providing estimated fares and ensuring reliable service.

- **XE Currency App:** Converts North Macedonian denar to your currency in real-time, helping you manage budget and transactions.

Chapter 6

Top Destinations And Tourist Must-Visit Attractions

Skopje: City Highlights and Main Sights

My Experience

Skopje is a city that immediately immerses you in contrasts: towering modern monuments, bridges, and sculptures stand side-by-side with Ottoman-era mosques and bazaars. The blend of architecture from different eras, including recent statues and neoclassical-style buildings, creates a unique and sometimes surreal experience. Walking through the Old Bazaar is a journey back in time with vibrant markets, tea shops, and a bustling energy that represents the city's rich heritage.

Historical View

Skopje has been inhabited since ancient times and has seen Roman, Byzantine, and Ottoman influence. The famous Stone Bridge, dating back to the 6th century, is an iconic link between Skopje's old and new parts. After a massive earthquake in 1963, Skopje underwent significant reconstruction, leading to the city's current mix of architectural styles.

Must-See Attractions

1. Macedonia Square - Central square with the "Warrior on a Horse" statue.
2. Stone Bridge - Ancient bridge connecting the Old Bazaar and Macedonia Square.
3. Kale Fortress - Offering panoramic city views.
4. Old Bazaar - Historical marketplace with Ottoman-era buildings.
5. Mother Teresa Memorial House - Honoring Skopje-born Mother Teresa.

Location & How to Get There

- **Address:** Macedonia Square, Skopje 1000, North Macedonia
- **Directions:** From Skopje International Airport, it's a 25-minute drive or taxi ride to the city center.

Top Hotels in Skopje
Luxury Hotels:

1. **Hotel Marriott Skopje** - Plostad Makedonija 7, Skopje | [Website](https://www.marriott.com) | $130–$200 per night | Spa, rooftop pool, fitness center
2. **Bushi Resort & Spa** - Samoilova 1, Skopje | [Website](https://www.bushiresort.com.mk) | $120–$170 per night | Spa, hammam, pool, restaurant
3. **DoubleTree by Hilton Skopje** - Blvd. ASNOM 17, Skopje | [Website](https://www.hilton.com) | $110–$150 per night | Indoor pool, spa
4. **Park Hotel & Spa** - 1732 Str. No. 4, Skopje | [Website](https://www.parkhotel.mk) | $100–$140 per night | Spa, gym
5. **Limak Skopje Luxury Hotel** - Str. Jordan Mijalkov, Skopje | [Website](https://www.limakskopje.com) | $90–$130 per night | Turkish bath, rooftop dining

Mid-Range Hotels:
1. **Hotel Solun & Spa** - Nikola Vapcarov 10, Skopje | [Website](https://www.hotelsolun.com.mk) | $70–$90 per night | Eco-friendly, breakfast buffet
2. **Ibis Skopje City Center** - Orce Nikolov 55, Skopje | [Website](https://all.accor.com) | $60–$80 per night | Terrace bar, 24-hour service
3. **Hotel City Park** - 8 Udarna Brigada 31, Skopje | [Website](https://www.cityparkhotel.mk) | $70–$90 per night | Free parking, bar
4. **Hostel Atlantik Skopje** - Anton Popov 9, Skopje | [Website](https://www.hostelatlantik.com.mk) | $40–$60 per night | Shared kitchen

5. Kapistec Hotel - Mile Pop Jordanov 3, Skopje | [Website](https://www.hotelkapistec.com.mk) | $50–$70 per night | Free Wi-Fi, terrace

Ohrid: Lake, Old Town, and UNESCO Heritage Sites

My Experience
Ohrid is breathtaking, with its serene lake views, historic churches, and cobblestone streets. Exploring the Old Town feels like stepping into another era, with narrow lanes leading to ancient churches and viewpoints over Lake Ohrid's crystal-clear waters. A boat ride on the lake during sunset is an unforgettable experience.

Historical View
Ohrid's history spans over two millennia. Known as the "Jerusalem of the Balkans," it boasts an impressive collection of medieval churches. Ohrid was also a key center for Slavic

literacy and culture, with the Ohrid Literary School founded by Saint Clement in the 9th century. The entire city is listed as a UNESCO World Heritage Site.

Must-See Attractions
1. Lake Ohrid - One of Europe's oldest and deepest lakes.
2. Samuel's Fortress - Offering panoramic views over Ohrid.
3. Church of St. John at Kaneo - Picturesque church overlooking the lake.
4. Saint Panteleimon Monastery - Important historical and religious site.
5. Ancient Theatre of Ohrid - Roman theater with concerts and events.

Location & How to Get There
- **Address:** Ohrid 6000, North Macedonia
- **Directions:** A 3-hour bus or car ride from Skopje. Ohrid also has an international airport with flights from European cities.

Top Hotels in Ohrid
Luxury Hotels:
1. Hotel Tino Sveti Stefan - Nas. Sveti Stefan BB, Ohrid | [Website](https://www.hoteltino.mk) | $100–$150 per night | Spa, pool
2. Inex Gorica Ohrid - Naum Ohridski 5-7, Ohrid | [Website](https://www.inexgorica.mk) | $110–$160 per night | Private beach, sauna

3. **Aleksandar Villa & Spa** - Nas. Konjsko BB, Ohrid | [Website](https://www.aleksandarvilla.com.mk) | $120–$180 per night | Spa, garden
4. **SU Hotel** - Kej Marsal Tito 91 A, Ohrid | [Website](https://www.su-hotel.com) | $90–$130 per night | Lake views, restaurant
5. **Hotel Belvedere Ohrid** - Nas. Sveti Stefan, Ohrid | [Website](https://www.hotelbelvedere.com.mk) | $80–$120 per night | Fitness center

Mid-Range Hotels:
1. **Villa & Winery Mal Sveti Kliment** - Kaneo 3, Ohrid | [Website](https://www.malsvetikliment.com) | $60–$80 per night | Boutique stay, breakfast included
2. **Hotel Vila Sofija** - Kosta Abras 64, Ohrid | [Website](https://www.vilasofija.com.mk) | $70–$90 per night | Courtyard, lake views
3. **Hotel Lebed Ohrid** - Kej Makedonija 97, Ohrid | [Website](https://www.hotellebedohrid.mk) | $65–$85 per night | Terrace bar
4. **Villa St. Sofija** - Klimentov Univerzitet 27, Ohrid | [Website](https://www.villastsofia.com.mk) | $60–$80 per night | Traditional decor
5. **Villa Mesokastro** - Braka Miladinovci 59, Ohrid | [Website](https://www.villamesokastro.com.mk) | $50–$70 per night | Lake views

Bitola: Historical Gems and Cultural Spots

My Experience

Bitola, known as the "City of Consuls," is full of charm, with Ottoman-era buildings, colorful streets, and a historic center rich in architecture. I enjoyed walking along the Shirok Sokak pedestrian street, filled with cafes, boutiques, and impressive buildings. Bitola has a relaxed atmosphere with many spots to explore, making it a fantastic destination for history and culture lovers.

Historical View

Bitola has a deep historical significance, having been a prominent city during the Ottoman Empire. It was a hub for diplomacy and trade, hence the name "City of Consuls." The city also played an essential role in the Balkan wars and retains several historic consulates, mosques, and ancient ruins, giving visitors a glimpse into its illustrious past.

Must-See Attractions
1. Shirok Sokak Street - Main pedestrian street with cafes and shops.
2. Heraclea Lyncestis - Ancient city founded by Philip II of Macedon.
3. Bitola Clock Tower - A famous Ottoman-era landmark.
4. Church of St. Dimitrija - Known for its rich frescoes.
5. National Museum of Bitola - Showcasing Bitola's history and cultural heritage.

Location & How to Get There
- **Address:** Bitola, North Macedonia
- **Directions:** Bitola is about a 2-hour drive from Skopje. Buses are also available from the main bus station in Skopje.

Top Hotels in Bitola
Luxury Hotels:
1. Hotel Epinal - Shirok Sokak 62, Bitola | [Website](https://www.epinal.com.mk) | $90–$130 per night | Spa, casino, indoor pool
2. Millenium Palace Hotel - Marshal Tito 48, Bitola | [Website](https://www.millenium.com.mk) | $80–$120 per night | Fitness center, terrace
3. Hotel Theatre - 10 Marshal Tito, Bitola | [Website](https://www.hoteltheatre.mk) | $70–$100 per night | On-site restaurant, modern decor

4. Sumski Feneri Hotel - 1 Trnovo Village, Bitola | [Website](https://www.sumski.mk) | $80–$110 per night | Garden views, traditional Macedonian decor

5. Premier Centar Hotel - Shirok Sokak 82, Bitola | [Website](https://www.premiercentar.mk) | $85–$115 per night | Cozy, centrally located

Mid-Range Hotels:

1. Hotel Ambasador Bitola - Solunska 137, Bitola | [Website](https://www.hotelambasador.mk) | $50–$70 per night | Convenient location, modern amenities

2. Villa Dihovo - Dihovo Village, Bitola | [Website](https://www.villadihovo.com.mk) | $40–$60 per night | Rustic charm, local cuisine

3. Hotel Kapri - 14 Vasko Karangeleski, Bitola | [Website](https://www.hotelkapri.mk) | $60–$80 per night | Free Wi-Fi, restaurant

4. Hotel Tokin House - Stiv Naumov 80, Bitola | [Website](https://www.tokinhouse.mk) | $55–$75 per night | Traditional architecture, central location

5. Hotel Theatre Central - Shirok Sokak 64, Bitola | [Website](https://www.hoteltheatre.mk) | $60–$85 per night | Cozy, well-located

Mavrovo National Park and Outdoor Escapes

My Experience
Mavrovo National Park is a nature lover's paradise. From scenic trails and lakes to winter ski slopes, it's a great escape from the city. Hiking along the park's trails and seeing Mavrovo Lake surrounded by mountains was one of the most peaceful experiences of my trip. If you enjoy nature, wildlife, and outdoor activities, Mavrovo is a must-visit.

Historical View
Mavrovo National Park, established in 1949, covers over 700 square kilometers of protected forests, rivers, and meadows. It's home to Macedonia's highest peak, Mount Korab, and serves as a sanctuary for various species like the lynx and brown bear. The park also has cultural importance, with the submerged Church of St. Nicholas, visible above Mavrovo Lake depending on water levels.

Must-See Attractions

1. **Mavrovo Lake** - Artificial lake with the submerged Church of St. Nicholas.
2. **Galicnik Village** - Known for traditional Macedonian architecture and the Galicnik Wedding Festival.
3. **Mount Korab** - Macedonia's highest peak, popular for hiking.
4. **St. Jovan Bigorski Monastery** - 11th-century monastery with stunning iconostasis.
5. **Ski Mavrovo** - Top destination for winter sports enthusiasts.

Location & How to Get There
- **Address:** Mavrovo National Park, North Macedonia
- Directions: About a 1.5-hour drive from Skopje by car. Buses from Skopje to Mavrovo are also available.

Top Hotels Near Mavrovo National Park
Luxury Hotels:
1. **Hotel Radika Resort & Spa** - Mavrovo, Mavrovo | [Website](https://www.radika.com.mk) | $120–$180 per night | Spa, indoor pool, restaurant
2. **Hotel Makpetrol Mavrovo** - Mavrovo Village | [Website](https://www.makpetrol.com.mk) | $110–$160 per night | Lake views, gym
3. **Bistra Hotel** - Mavrovo, Mavrovo | [Website](https://www.hotelbistra.mk) | $90–$130 per night | Indoor pool, terrace
4. **Hotel Korab Trnica** - Trnica Village, Mavrovo | [Website](https://www.korabtrnica.com) | $100–$140 per night | Mountain views, traditional decor

5. **Hotel Alpina Mavrovo** - Mavrovo Village | [Website](https://www.alpinamavrovo.mk) | $95–$125 per night | Ski-in/ski-out access

Mid-Range Hotels:
1. **Hotel Srna Mavrovo** - Mavrovo, Mavrovo | [Website](https://www.hotelsrna.mk) | $60–$80 per night | Family-friendly, nearby trails
2. **Villa Mavrovo** - Mavrovo Village | [Website](https://www.villamavrovo.com) | $50–$70 per night | Cozy, budget-friendly
3. **Hotel Golden Place** - Mavrovo, Mavrovo | [Website](https://www.goldplace.mk) | $70–$90 per night | Views of Mavrovo Lake
4. **Hotel Sator** - Mavrovo, Mavrovo | [Website](https://www.hotelsator.mk) | $60–$85 per night | Restaurant, Wi-Fi
5. **Villa Flora Mavrovo** - Mavrovo Village | [Website](https://www.villaflora.mk) | $55–$75 per night | Modern decor, lake views

Other Must-See Cities, Towns, and Villages

North Macedonia has several charming towns and villages beyond the well-known destinations of Skopje, Ohrid, and Bitola. Each of these places offers unique experiences, historical depth, and cultural insights.

My Experience
Exploring these smaller towns gave me a deeper connection to North Macedonia's traditions and lifestyle. Each town has its unique pace and flavor, making for authentic and intimate travel experiences. Visiting villages like Krusevo, with its hilltop charm, and Vevčani, famous for its annual carnival, provided cultural moments I won't forget.

Historical View
North Macedonia's smaller cities and villages are often steeped in centuries-old traditions. Towns like Krusevo played key roles in historical uprisings, while others, like Vevčani, are celebrated for their cultural festivities. Many of these

towns are set against breathtaking landscapes, with architecture reflecting Ottoman, Byzantine, and Slavic influences.

Must-See Attractions
1. **Krusevo** - Highest town in North Macedonia, known for the Ilinden Uprising monument.
2. **Vevčani** - Famous for the Vevčani Carnival and natural springs.
3. **Struga** - A town on Lake Ohrid's shore with a vibrant poetry festival.
4. **Berovo** - Known for its serene Berovo Lake and organic honey production.
5. **Prilep** - Famous for its tobacco industry and medieval monasteries.

Location & How to Get There
- **Address:** Various towns across North Macedonia
- **Directions:** Many of these towns are accessible by bus from Skopje or Ohrid. Car rentals are also a convenient option for traveling between these locations.

Top Hotels in Key Towns
Luxury Hotels:
1. **Hotel Montana Palace (Krusevo)** - Krusevo 7550 | [Website](https://www.montanapalace.mk) | $80–$120 per night | Hilltop views, restaurant, gym
2. **Hotel Tutto (Berovo)** - Berovo Lake, Berovo | [Website](https://www.hoteltutto.mk) | $90–$130 per night | Lake views, traditional decor

3. **Hotel Drim (Struga)** - Kej Boris Kidric 51, Struga | [Website](https://www.hoteldrim.mk) | $100–$150 per night | Lakefront location, pool

4. **Hotel Kristal Palas (Prilep)** - Edvard Kardelj 240, Prilep | [Website](https://www.kristalpalas.mk) | $90–$130 per night | Gym, terrace, local cuisine

5. **Aurora Resort & Spa (Berovo)** - Ul. 3, Berovo | [Website](https://www.aurora.mk) | $110–$160 per night | Spa, mountain views

Mid-Range Hotels:

1. **Hotel Krusevo (Krusevo)** - Krusevo, 7550 | [Website](https://www.hotelkrusevo.mk) | $50–$70 per night | Central location, local dining

2. **Hotel Royal (Struga)** - Radozda Village, Struga | [Website](https://www.hotelroyal.mk) | $60–$80 per night | Lake views, budget-friendly

3. **Villa Bella (Berovo)** - Berovo, North Macedonia | [Website](https://www.villabella.mk) | $55–$75 per night | Rustic charm, great views

4. **Hotel Makedonija (Prilep)** - Prilep, North Macedonia | [Website](https://www.makedonija.mk) | $65–$85 per night | Cozy rooms, cafe

5. **Vila Kaliakra (Vevčani)** - Vevčani, North Macedonia | [Website](https://www.vilakaliakra.mk) | $50–$70 per night | Traditional Vevčani decor, local charm

Kokino Observatory

My Experience

Visiting Kokino was an otherworldly experience, as this ancient observatory offers breathtaking views and a chance to witness one of the oldest astronomical sites in the world. Standing on the rocks where people observed the stars millennia ago connected me deeply with the history and mysteries of ancient Macedonia.

Historical View

Kokino, dating back over 3,800 years, is considered one of the world's oldest observatories, alongside sites like Stonehenge. It was used by the Bronze Age inhabitants of the region to track lunar and solar cycles, making it a UNESCO-recognized cultural heritage site and a must-visit for history and astronomy enthusiasts.

Must-See Features

1. **Observation Platform** - Stone seats where ancient observers watched the sky.
2. **Sun Gates** - Openings used to track the sun's movement.
3. **Panoramic Views** - Overlooking the surrounding landscapes, perfect for stargazing.

Location & How to Get There
- **Address:** Kokino, Staro Nagorichane Municipality, North Macedonia
- **Directions:** Located about 75 km from Skopje, accessible by car. Local guides are available.

Top Hotels Near Kokino Observatory
Luxury Hotels:
1. **Hotel Stone Age** - Near Kokino, Staro Nagorichane | [Website](https://www.hotelstoneage.mk) | $85–$120 per night | Rustic decor, astronomical themes
2. **Hotel Royal View (Kumanovo)** - Near Kokino | [Website](https://www.hotelroyalview.mk) | $100–$140 per night | Views, pool, restaurant
3. **Etno Selo Hotel (Kumanovo)** - Near Kokino | [Website](https://www.etnoselo.mk) | $90–$130 per night | Traditional architecture, peaceful ambiance
4. **TCC Plaza Hotel (Skopje)** - Skopje, near Kokino | [Website](https://www.tccplaza.mk) | $110–$150 per night | Pool, fitness center
5. **Hotel Oaza** (Staro Nagorichane) | [Website](https://www.hoteloaza.mk) | $100–$130 per night | Natural setting, nearby tours

Mid-Range Hotels:
1. **Hotel Gradce (Kumanovo)** - Near Kokino | [Website](https://www.hotelgradce.mk) | $60–$80 per night | Family-friendly, restaurant
2. **Villa Rock** - Kumanovo | [Website](https://www.villarock.mk) | $50–$70 per night | Basic amenities, good location
3. **Guesthouse Nagorichane** - Staro Nagorichane | [Website](https://www.guesthousenagorichane.mk) | $45–$65 per night | Budget-friendly, quiet
4. **Hotel Brioni** - Kumanovo | [Website](https://www.hotelbrioni.mk) | $55–$75 per night | Simple decor, great hospitality
5. Villa Kokino - Near Kokino Observatory | [Website](https://www.villakokino.mk) | $50–$70 per night | Close to the site, cozy ambiance

Heraclea Lyncestis

My Experience
Visiting Heraclea Lyncestis was like stepping back in time. Walking among ancient mosaics, Roman baths, and basilicas, I felt an awe for the craftsmanship and history that spanned from the ancient Macedonian era through Roman rule. This site offers an immersive glimpse into North Macedonia's rich classical history.

Historical View
Founded in the 4th century BC by Philip II of Macedon, Heraclea Lyncestis was an important city in the ancient Macedonian kingdom. It later flourished under Roman rule, becoming a crucial center along the Via Egnatia trade route. Today, the site's intricate mosaics, theater, and basilica ruins reflect its classical heritage, attracting history enthusiasts from around the world.

Must-See Features
1. Roman Theatre - A well-preserved amphitheater still used for performances.
2. Mosaics - Detailed floor mosaics showcasing scenes from mythology.
3. Basilica Ruins - Remains of the basilica walls with early Christian art.

Location & How to Get There
- **Address:** Heraclea Lyncestis, Bitola, North Macedonia
- **Directions:** Located just 2 km from Bitola's city center, accessible by car or taxi.

Top Hotels Near Heraclea Lyncestis
Luxury Hotels:
1. Hotel Epinal - Shirok Sokak 62, Bitola | [Website](https://www.hotelepinal.mk) | $100–$140 per night | Spa, pool, fitness center
2. Hotel Millenium Palace - Marshal Tito 48, Bitola | [Website](https://www.millenium.mk) | $110–$150 per night | Elegant rooms, onsite restaurant
3. Hotel Ambasador - Bitola | [Website](https://www.ambasador.mk) | $95–$130 per night | Central location, modern decor
4. Hotel Theatre - Leninova 97, Bitola | [Website](https://www.hoteltheatre.mk) | $90–$130 per night | Stylish rooms, close to attractions
5. Hotel Sator - Magarevo Village, Bitola | [Website](https://www.hotelsator.mk) | $110–$160 per night | Mountain views, peaceful setting

Mid-Range Hotels:
1. Villa Diamond - Bitola |
[Website](https://www.villadiamond.mk) | $60–$80 per night | Comfort rooms, local atmosphere
2. Chola Guest House - Stiv Naumov St, Bitola | [Website](https://www.cholaguesthouse.mk) | $55–$75 per night | Traditional decor, cozy ambiance
3. **Villa Konzuli -** Shirok Sokak, Bitola | [Website](https://www.villakonzuli.mk) | $50–$70 per night | Boutique style, historical charm
4. **Hotel Korzo** - Bitola | [Website](https://www.hotelkorzo.mk) | $50–$65 per night | Central location, good value
5. **Hostel Domestika -** Bitola | [Website](https://www.hosteldomestika.mk) | $45–$60 per night | Affordable, friendly staff

Stobi Archaeological Site

My Experience

Exploring Stobi was like piecing together fragments of history. Known for its impressive mosaics, ancient streets, and remnants of early Christian basilicas, Stobi offers a profound insight into North Macedonia's Roman and Byzantine past. It was fascinating to imagine life in this once-thriving city.

Historical View

Stobi, situated at the confluence of the Crna and Vardar rivers, was one of the most significant cities in the ancient Macedonian and later Roman Empire. Known for its advanced urban planning, it hosted luxurious houses, a theater, temples, and churches. Stobi provides valuable insights into ancient Roman and early Christian architecture.

Must-See Features
1. **Roman Amphitheatre** - Large arena with impressive acoustics.
2. **Theodosian Palace** - Lavish residence with intricate mosaics.
3. **Basilicas** - Early Christian churches showcasing religious mosaics.

Location & How to Get There
- **Address:** Gradsko, North Macedonia
- **Directions:** Located about 80 km from Skopje, reachable by car or bus. Tours are available from major cities.

Top Hotels Near Stobi
Luxury Hotels:
1. **Gardenia Hotel & Spa** - Veles, North Macedonia | [Website](https://www.hotelgardenia.mk) | $100–$140 per night | Spa, outdoor pool
2. **Hotel Mirror** - Near Skopje Airport | [Website](https://www.hotelmirror.mk) | $90–$130 per night | Convenient for airport access
3. **Hotel Glam** - Veles | [Website](https://www.hotelglam.mk) | $95–$135 per night | Stylish decor, good dining
4. **Hotel Romantique** - Veles Lake | [Website](https://www.romantique.mk) | $110–$150 per night | Lakeside views, relaxing ambiance

5. Hotel International - Skopje | [Website](https://www.hotelinternational.mk) | $100–$140 per night | City views, contemporary style

Mid-Range Hotels:
1. Villa Stobi - Gradsko | [Website](https://www.villastobi.mk) | $60–$80 per night | Close to the archaeological site
2. Villa Zora - Near Stobi | [Website](https://www.villazora.mk) | $50–$70 per night | Countryside ambiance
3. Hotel Park - Veles | [Website](https://www.hotelpark.mk) | $55–$75 per night | Comfortable rooms, central
4. Guest House Stobi - Gradsko | [Website](https://www.guesthousestobi.mk) | $50–$65 per night | Traditional decor, affordable
5. Hostel River - Veles | [Website](https://www.hostelriver.mk) | $45–$60 per night | Budget-friendly, good amenities

Marko's Towers (Markovi Kuli)

My Experience

Hiking up to Marko's Towers was an invigorating experience. With panoramic views and the remnants of medieval fortifications, I felt immersed in the folklore surrounding King Marko. The climb was worth it for both the historical insight and the breathtaking landscape.

Historical View

Marko's Towers are remnants of a fortress built during the 13th century, associated with the legendary Serbian King Marko. Located in the town of Prilep, the site offers insight into medieval fortification techniques and the region's turbulent history.

Must-See Features

1. Fortress Ruins - Medieval stone towers and walls.
2. Scenic Views - Panoramic views of Prilep and surrounding landscapes.
3. Hiking Trails - Nature trails leading up to the towers.

Location & How to Get There

- **Address:** Prilep, North Macedonia
- **Directions:** Accessible by a short drive and hike from Prilep's center. Guided hikes are available.

Top Hotels Near Marko's Towers

Luxury Hotels:
1. Hotel Kristal Palas - Prilep | [Website](https://www.kristalpalas.mk) | $90–$130 per night | Terrace, fitness center
2. Hotel Salida - Prilep | [Website](https://www.hotelsalida.mk) | $100–$140 per night | Modern decor, restaurant
3. Hotel Ambasador - Near Prilep | [Website](https://www.ambasador.mk) | $95–$130 per night | Central location, modern rooms

4. **Hotel Atlas** - Prilep | [Website](https://www.hotelatlas.mk) | $100–$140 per night | Stylish, comfortable
5. **Hotel Breza** - Prilep | [Website](https://www.hotelbreza.mk) | $85–$120 per night | Cozy, great views

Mid-Range Hotels:
1. **Hotel Sonce** - Prilep | [Website](https://www.hotelsonce.mk) | $60–$80 per night | Great value, comfortable rooms
2. **Villa Prilep** - Prilep | [Website](https://www.villaprilep.mk) | $55–$75 per night | Traditional style, cozy
3. **Hotel La Ponderosa** - Prilep | [Website](https://www.hotellaponderosa.mk) | $50–$70 per night | Budget-friendly, convenient
4. **Guesthouse Mira** - Prilep | [Website](https://www.guesthousemira.mk) | $45–$65 per night | Friendly, clean
5. **Villa Golden Gate** - Prilep | [Website](https://www.villagoldengate.mk) | $50–$65 per night | Homely ambiance

Tikveš Wine Region

My Experience
The Tikveš Wine Region is an absolute delight for wine enthusiasts. During my visit, I experienced the charm of traditional Macedonian wine-making firsthand. Strolling through vineyards, sampling local wines, and learning about the rich history of winemaking in North Macedonia made it a memorable experience. The hospitality at the wineries was warm, with sommeliers sharing the unique flavors and techniques behind each bottle.

Historical View
The Tikveš Wine Region is the heart of North Macedonia's wine country and has a history dating back more than 2,000 years. Known for its ideal climate and fertile soil, the region produces a variety of high-quality wines, especially reds like Vranec. Influenced by both Mediterranean and continental weather, Tikveš has become renowned for traditional

winemaking practices mixed with modern innovation, placing it among the oldest and most significant wine-producing areas in the Balkans.

Must-See Wineries and Attractions
1. Tikveš Winery - The oldest and most famous winery in North Macedonia.
2. Popova Kula Winery - Known for its wine-tasting experiences and views.
3. Stobi Winery - Offers tours showcasing traditional and modern wine production techniques.

Location & How to Get There
- **Address:** Tikveš Wine Region, Kavadarci, North Macedonia
- **Directions:** Located near the town of Kavadarci, the region is about a 1.5-hour drive from Skopje. Many wineries offer tours, which can be pre-booked.

Top Hotels Near the Tikveš Wine Region
Luxury Hotels:
1. Hotel Uni Palas - Aleksandar Makedonski Blvd, Kavadarci | [Website](https://www.hotelunipalas.mk) | $110–$150 per night | Rooftop bar, spacious rooms, central location.
2. Popova Kula Hotel - Demir Kapija | [Website](https://www.popovakula.com.mk) | $100–$140 per night | Winery hotel, panoramic views, wine tours.
3. Hotel Feni - Ilindenska St, Kavadarci | [Website](https://www.hotelfeni.mk) | $90–$130 per night | Modern decor, wellness services.

4. Villa Bella Boutique - Kavadarci |
[Website](https://www.villabellaboutique.mk) | $120–$160 per night | Boutique style, excellent service, on-site restaurant.
5. Hotel Nar - Gevgelija |
[Website](https://www.hotelnar.mk) | $100–$140 per night | Elegant rooms, pool, close to vineyards.

Mid-Range Hotels:
1. Hotel Bozur - Kavadarci |
[Website](https://www.hotelbozur.mk) | $60–$85 per night | Cozy rooms, local charm.
2. Guest House Vinska - Near Kavadarci |
[Website](https://www.guesthousevinska.mk) | $55–$75 per night | Countryside ambiance, friendly hosts.
3. Villa Vino - Kavadarci |
[Website](https://www.villavino.mk) | $65–$85 per night | Ideal for wine enthusiasts, homely environment.
4. Hotel Kavadarci - Kavadarci Center |
[Website](https://www.hotelkavadarci.mk) | $50–$70 per night | Basic amenities, great location.
5. Hostel Vino - Kavadarci |
[Website](https://www.hostelvino.mk) | $40–$60 per night | Affordable, communal atmosphere, near wineries.

Chapter 7

Hidden Gems and Off-the-Beaten-Path Adventures

Lesser-Known Historic Sites

My Experience

Exploring North Macedonia's lesser-known historic sites was a journey filled with surprises. Each location revealed stories that are often overshadowed by the more famous attractions. I particularly enjoyed the quiet atmosphere of these sites, where I could reflect on the rich history and cultural heritage without the crowds. The local guides were enthusiastic and shared captivating tales that added depth to my visit.

Historical View

North Macedonia is dotted with historic sites that tell the story of its complex past, influenced by various civilizations, including the Romans, Ottomans, and Byzantines. These lesser-known sites often highlight the everyday lives of people from different eras, showcasing architectural styles, religious influences, and local traditions that have evolved over time.

Must-See Lesser-Known Historic Sites

1. Heraclea Lyncestis - Ancient city with Roman ruins near Bitola.
   - **Address:** Heraclea, near Bitola, North Macedonia
   - **How to Get There:** A short drive from Bitola; follow signs to the archaeological site.

2. Markovi Kuli (Marko's Towers) - Medieval fortress offering stunning views.
   - **Address:** Near Prilep, North Macedonia
   - **How to Get There:** Accessible via a short hike from Prilep.

3. Kokino Observatory - Ancient astronomical site.
   - **Address:** Near the village of Staro Nagoričane
   - **How to Get There:** A drive from Skopje followed by a short hike.

Top Hotels Near Lesser-Known Historic Sites
Luxury Hotels:

1. Hotel Epinal - 4 Blagoja Parovića St, Bitola |
[Website](https://www.hotelepinal.com) | $90–$130 per night | Modern amenities, spa, close to historical sites.
2. Hotel Aleksandar Palace - 3-5, Dime Dinev St, Skopje |
[Website](https://www.hotelaleksandar.mk) | $100–$150 per night | Luxurious rooms, great views, near city center.
3. Hotel Tino - St. Sveti Kliment Ohridski 33, Ohrid |
[Website](https://www.hoteltino.com.mk) | $80–$120 per night | Lakeside views, restaurant, perfect for exploring.
4. Hotel Granit - Ohrid |
[Website](https://www.hotelgranit.mk) | $70–$100 per night | Beachfront, outdoor pool, near ancient sites.
5. Hotel Sanja - Prilep |
[Website](https://www.hotelsanja.mk) | $75–$110 per night | Comfortable, close to Marko's Towers.

Mid-Range Hotels:
1. Hotel Makedonija - Bitola |
[Website](https://www.hotelmakedonija.mk) | $55–$80 per night | Convenient location, cozy atmosphere.
2. Hotel Templum - Prilep |
[Website](https://www.hotelsanja.mk) | $50–$70 per night | Simple yet comfortable, near Markovi Kuli.
3. Villa St. Kliment - Ohrid |
[Website](https://www.villastkliment.com) | $40–$65 per night | Close to Lake Ohrid, homely feel.
4. Hotel City Park - Skopje |
[Website](https://www.hotelcitypark.mk) | $60–$85 per night | Central location, friendly service.

5. Hotel Kristal - Bitola |
[Website](https://www.hotelkristal.mk) | $45–$70 per night | Basic amenities, convenient for exploring.

Scenic Landscapes and Natural Wonders

Mavrovo National Park

- My Experience: Mavrovo National Park was a nature lover's paradise. Hiking through lush forests, I encountered diverse wildlife, pristine lakes, and breathtaking mountain views. I visited the famous Mavrovo Lake, where the submerged church spire peeks out of the water—a striking sight that lingers in memory.

- Overview: Mavrovo is the largest national park in North Macedonia, known for its stunning landscapes, outdoor activities (hiking, skiing), and rich biodiversity.

- Location & How to Get There:
  - **Address:** Mavrovo, North Macedonia

- **Directions:** Approximately 90 km from Skopje. Accessible by car via the A2 highway.

Lake Ohrid
- **My Experience:** My time at Lake Ohrid was serene and rejuvenating. The crystal-clear waters and the surrounding mountains made it a perfect spot for reflection. I also enjoyed a boat trip to explore hidden beaches and local fishing villages.
- **Overview:** Lake Ohrid is one of Europe's oldest and deepest lakes, a UNESCO World Heritage site, renowned for its biodiversity and stunning scenery.
- **Location & How to Get There:**
  - **Address:** Ohrid, North Macedonia
  - **Directions:** About 180 km from Skopje, easily reachable by bus or car along the E65 road.

Unique Local Experiences and Traditions

Traditional Macedonian Cuisine

- **My Experience:** Indulging in traditional Macedonian dishes was a highlight of my trip. I savored meals like Tavče Gravče (baked beans) and Ajvar (pepper spread), which were bursting with flavor. Dining at a local restaurant where the owner shared stories of family recipes added a personal touch to the experience.
- **Overview:** Macedonian cuisine reflects a blend of Mediterranean and Balkan flavors, emphasizing fresh ingredients and traditional cooking methods.
- **Recommendation:** Try visiting local taverns (kafana) in towns like Bitola or Skopje for authentic meals.

Cultural Festivals

- **My Experience:** I had the chance to attend the Ohrid Summer Festival, which showcased local music, dance, and art. The atmosphere was vibrant, with performances in the backdrop of stunning ancient churches and the lake. It was a wonderful way to engage with local culture and meet people.
- **Overview:** North Macedonia hosts numerous cultural festivals throughout the year, celebrating its rich traditions through music, dance, and art. Notable events include the Skopje Jazz Festival and the Vardar River Carnival.
- **Tips:** Check local calendars for festival dates, as they vary annually.

Chapter 8

Outdoor Activities and Adventure Sports

Hiking, Trekking, and Mountain Climbing

North Macedonia is a hiker's paradise, boasting diverse landscapes, breathtaking views, and well-marked trails. Here are some of the best spots for hiking and trekking:

- **National Park Mavrovo:**
  - **Trails:** The park features various trails suitable for all skill levels. Popular routes include the hike to the peak of Shar Mountain, which offers stunning views of the surrounding landscapes.

- **Highlights:** Mavrovo Lake and the iconic St. Jovan Bigorski Monastery.

- Pelister National Park:
- **Trails:** Offers trails that lead to the Pelister Peak (2,601 meters) and the beautiful Pelister Lakes (Macedonian: Pelisterski Oči).
- **Wildlife:** Home to endemic species like the Pelister Pygmy Goat and a variety of flora.

- Kuklica and the Stone Dolls:
- **Description:** This area is known for its natural rock formations resembling human figures. The hike to the site is both scenic and unique.

- Galičica National Park:
- **Trails:** Trails connect Lake Ohrid and Lake Prespa, allowing hikers to enjoy views of both lakes and diverse wildlife.
- **Wildlife:** Notable for its rich biodiversity, including rare species.

Tips for Hiking:
- **Best Time to Visit:** Spring and early autumn offer the best weather for hiking.
- **Gear:** Good hiking boots, plenty of water, and a map or GPS device are essential.
- **Local Guides:** Consider hiring local guides for specific trails, especially if you're unfamiliar with the terrain.

Lake Ohrid and Water Activities

Lake Ohrid, one of Europe's oldest and deepest lakes, is a UNESCO World Heritage Site known for its crystal-clear waters and diverse ecosystems.

- Swimming and Beaches:
   - Popular spots include Ohrid City Beach, Labino Beach, and Trpejca Beach. The water is clean and perfect for swimming in the summer months.

- Water Sports:
   - **Kayaking and Canoeing:** Rent a kayak to explore the lake at your own pace.
   - **Stand-Up Paddleboarding:** Available for those looking for a fun and active way to enjoy the water.

- Diving:

- **Diving Schools:** There are several diving schools offering courses and guided dives to explore underwater caves and ancient ruins.
- **Notable Sites:** The submerged Roman city and the many endemic fish species.

- Boat Tours:
- Take a boat tour to visit the picturesque towns of Ohrid, Struga, and Vevčani, and explore hidden beaches and coves.

- Fishing:
- Known for its trout, fishing in Lake Ohrid can be a relaxing way to spend a day. Ensure to check local regulations.

Tips for Lake Ohrid:
- **Season:** Summer (June to August) is peak season for water activities, with warm temperatures ideal for swimming and sunbathing.
- **Local Cuisine:** Don't miss trying local fish dishes, particularly the famous Ohrid trout.

Winter Sports: Skiing and Snowboarding

North Macedonia offers excellent opportunities for winter sports enthusiasts, especially in the mountainous regions.

- Mavrovo Ski Resort:
- **Location:** Situated in Mavrovo National Park, it's the largest ski resort in the country.
- **Facilities:** Offers a range of slopes for all skill levels, ski rentals, and ski schools for beginners.

- **Activities:** Besides skiing and snowboarding, visitors can enjoy snowshoeing and sledding.

- **Kopanki Ski Center:**
- **Location:** Near the town of Debar, this smaller ski area is ideal for families and less crowded.
 - **Features:** Suitable for beginners and offers a friendly atmosphere.

Tips for Winter Sports:
- **Season:** December to March is the best time for skiing and snowboarding.
- Equipment: Rentals are available at resorts, but bring your own gear for the best experience.

Nature Parks and Wildlife Exploration

North Macedonia is rich in biodiversity and offers numerous nature parks where travelers can explore unique flora and fauna.

- **National Park Pelister:**
  - **Wildlife:** Home to various animals, including bears, wolves, and many bird species.
  - **Flora:** Famous for its Macedonian pine trees and unique endemic plants.

- **Galičica National Park:**
  - **Activities:** Bird watching, photography, and exploring the diverse ecosystems from mountain peaks to lake shores.

- **Tikveš Lake:**
  - **Wildlife:** A great spot for birdwatching, particularly for migratory birds.
  - **Activities:** Fishing and picnicking around the scenic lake.

- **Demir Kapija:**
  - **Description:** Known for its stunning canyon and rock formations, it's an excellent place for rock climbing and hiking.

Tips for Wildlife Exploration:
- **Guided Tours:** Consider joining guided tours to learn more about the wildlife and conservation efforts.
- **Respect Nature:** Always follow park regulations and respect wildlife habitats.

Chapter 9

Culinary Experiences and Local Cuisine

Introduction to Macedonian Cuisine

Macedonian cuisine is a delightful blend of Mediterranean and Balkan influences, featuring fresh ingredients, vibrant flavors, and hearty portions. It reflects the country's diverse cultural heritage, with influences from Ottoman, Greek, and Slavic traditions.

Key Characteristics:
- **Seasonality:** Dishes are often prepared using seasonal and

locally sourced ingredients, including vegetables, meats, and dairy.
- **Flavor Profile:** Expect bold flavors from herbs and spices like paprika, garlic, and dill, often accompanied by olive oil and fresh bread.
- **Dining Experience:** Meals are typically communal, reflecting the hospitality of the Macedonian people. Sharing dishes is common and encouraged.

Must-Try Dishes and Local Specialties

North Macedonia boasts a variety of traditional dishes that are a must for any visitor:

- **Tavče Gravče:**
  - **Description:** A national dish of baked beans cooked with onions, peppers, and spices, traditionally served in a clay pot. It's hearty and perfect for vegetarians.
  - **Where to Try:** Many local taverns and restaurants serve this dish, especially in Ohrid.

- **Ajvar:**
  - **Description:** A flavorful roasted red pepper and eggplant spread. It's often served as a side dish or condiment.
  - **Serving Style:** Enjoyed with bread, grilled meats, or as part of a mezze platter.

- **Sarma:**
  - **Description:** Cabbage leaves stuffed with minced meat and rice, seasoned with spices and slowly cooked.

- **Regional Variants:** Each family may have its unique recipe, so trying different versions is a treat.

- Kebapi:
- **Description:** Grilled minced meat sausages, typically made from a mix of beef and lamb. They are served with onions and somun (flatbread).
- **Popular Spot:** Many restaurants in Skopje have their specialty kebapi.

- Grilled Fish:
- **Description:** Lake Ohrid is famous for its trout, which is often grilled and served with local vegetables and herbs.
- **Tip:** Fresh fish can be found at lakeside restaurants in Ohrid.

- Baklava:
- **Description:** A sweet pastry made of layers of filo dough, filled with nuts and sweetened with honey or syrup, reflecting Ottoman culinary influence.
- **Where to Find:** Try local bakeries or dessert shops for authentic baklava.

Best Restaurants, Cafes, and Street Food

North Macedonia has a vibrant food scene, from traditional restaurants to modern cafes:

- Restaurants:

- **Restaurant 22 (Skopje):** Known for its upscale take on traditional dishes and a cozy atmosphere. Signature dishes include Tavče Gravče and various grilled meats.
- **Stara Gradska Kafana (Skopje):** A charming restaurant offering authentic Macedonian fare in a traditional setting, famous for its Sarma and local wines.
- **Gino's (Ohrid):** A lakeside restaurant specializing in fresh fish and Mediterranean dishes with stunning views of Lake Ohrid.

- **Cafes:**
  - **Kino Kultura (Skopje):** A trendy café that serves great coffee and light snacks, often featuring cultural events and exhibitions.
  - **Café Guli (Ohrid):** A perfect spot for a coffee break with picturesque views of the lake.

- **Street Food:**
  - **Burek:** A flaky pastry filled with cheese, meat, or spinach, commonly found at bakeries and street vendors. It's a perfect on-the-go snack.
  - **Pita:** Another popular pastry, similar to burek but often filled with pumpkin or potatoes. Look for vendors selling these delights in local markets.

Wineries, Distilleries, and Beverage Culture

North Macedonia has a rich tradition of winemaking, thanks to its favorable climate and diverse grape varieties:

- **Wineries:**

- **Tikveš Winery:** One of the largest and most famous wineries in North Macedonia, known for its high-quality wines. They offer tours and tastings.
- **Skovin Winery:** Located near Lake Tikveš, Skovin produces both red and white wines and offers an excellent tasting experience.

- Local Varietals:
- **Vranec:** A rich red wine native to the region, known for its bold flavor and tannins.
- **Smederevka:** A white wine that pairs well with fish dishes and is appreciated for its light and fruity notes.

- Rakija:
- **Description:** A traditional fruit brandy, often made from plums or grapes. It is a staple at celebrations and meals.
- **Where to Try:** Distilleries often offer tastings, and many local restaurants serve homemade rakija as an aperitif.

Food Markets and Traditional Cooking Classes

Exploring local markets and participating in cooking classes are great ways to immerse yourself in Macedonian culture:

- Food Markets:
- **Bunjakovec Market (Skopje):** A bustling market offering fresh produce, meats, cheeses, and local delicacies. It's a great place to sample local products.

- **Old Bazaar (Skopje):** This historic market area is full of shops selling spices, sweets, and handmade goods. A perfect spot to find unique culinary souvenirs.

- Traditional Cooking Classes:

- **Cooking with Anna:** A popular cooking class in Ohrid that teaches participants to prepare traditional dishes like Sarma and Ajvar, using local ingredients.

- **Taste of Macedonia:** Offers cooking workshops where you can learn to make popular dishes while enjoying local wines. Classes often include a market visit to buy ingredients.

Chapter 10

Accommodation Options

Luxury Hotels and Resorts

North Macedonia offers several luxurious accommodations that provide top-notch amenities and stunning views.

- Alexander Palace Hotel (Skopje)
  - **Description:** A five-star hotel featuring elegantly designed rooms, a spa, and gourmet dining options. It is located close to the city center, making it ideal for exploring Skopje.
  - **Amenities:** Indoor pool, fitness center, wellness spa, and a rooftop restaurant with city views.
  - Contact Information:

- **Website:** [Alexander Palace Hotel](http://www.alexanderpalace.mk/)
  - **Phone:** +389 2 309 7777

- Villa & Winery Tikveš (Kavadarci)
  - **Description:** A luxurious winery and hotel situated in the picturesque Tikveš wine region. Guests can enjoy vineyard tours, wine tastings, and exquisite dining.
  - **Amenities:** Spacious suites, outdoor pool, and fine dining with a focus on local cuisine and wines.
  - **Contact Information:**
  - **Website:** [Villa & Winery Tikveš](https://www.villaandwinerytikves.com/)
  - **Phone:** +389 43 414 373

- **Hotel Granit (Ohrid)**
  - **Description:** A luxurious lakeside hotel offering stunning views of Lake Ohrid, spacious rooms, and excellent service.
  - **Amenities:** Private beach, wellness center, outdoor swimming pool, and various dining options.
  - **Contact Information:**
  - **Website:** [Hotel Granit](http://www.hotelgranit.mk/)
  - **Phone:** +389 46 266 700

Budget-Friendly Stays and Hostels

For budget-conscious travelers, North Macedonia offers several affordable options without compromising on comfort.

- **Hostel Skopje (Skopje)**

- **Description:** A modern hostel located in the city center, ideal for backpackers and solo travelers. It features a vibrant atmosphere and communal spaces.
  - **Amenities:** Free Wi-Fi, kitchen facilities, organized tours, and a bar.
  - **Contact Information:**
    - **Website:** [Hostel Skopje](https://www.hostelskopje.com/)
    - **Phone:** +389 76 229 900

- **Shanti Hostel (Skopje)**
  - **Description:** A cozy and friendly hostel that offers dormitory and private rooms. It's located near major attractions and has a relaxed vibe.
  - **Amenities:** Free breakfast, common lounge area, and travel assistance.
  - **Contact Information:**
    - **Website:** [Shanti Hostel](http://www.shantihostel.com/)
    - **Phone:** +389 2 322 6966

- **Villa Bune (Ohrid)**
  - **Description:** A budget-friendly guesthouse with simple but comfortable accommodations located close to the lake and town center.
  - **Amenities:** Free parking, garden area, and a shared kitchen.
  - **Contact Information:**
    - **Phone:** +389 46 261 300

Boutique Hotels and Traditional Guesthouses

For a more personalized experience, boutique hotels and guesthouses offer unique charm and character.

- Hotel Senigallia (Skopje)

- **Description:** A boutique hotel located on the banks of the Vardar River, featuring stylish decor and a relaxing atmosphere.
- **Amenities:** Restaurant, bar, and a terrace with river views.
- **Contact Information:**
- **Website:** [Hotel Senigallia](http://www.hotelsenigallia.com/)
- **Phone:** +389 2 323 5300

- Villa Old Town (Ohrid)

- **Description:** A beautifully renovated guesthouse located in the historic part of Ohrid, offering comfortable rooms with traditional décor.
- **Amenities:** Complimentary breakfast, garden, and a cozy lounge area.
- **Contact Information:**
- **Website:** [Villa Old Town](http://www.villaoldtown.com/)
- **Phone:** +389 46 262 702

- The Vineyards (Tikveš)

- **Description:** A boutique hotel set in a vineyard, providing a tranquil setting and beautiful surroundings for relaxation.
- **Amenities:** Wine tasting, fine dining, and stunning views of the vineyards.
- **Contact Information:**

- **Website:** [The Vineyards](https://thevineyards.mk/)
- **Phone:** +389 43 419 199

Tips for Booking

- **Plan Ahead:** Book accommodations in advance, especially during peak travel seasons (spring and summer) or for major holidays.
- **Check Reviews:** Use platforms like TripAdvisor, Booking.com, and Google Reviews to read about other travelers' experiences.
- **Consider Location:** Choose a place close to major attractions or public transport for convenience.
- **Look for Deals:** Check hotel websites for promotions or special packages that include meals or activities.
- **Contact Directly:** Sometimes, contacting hotels directly can lead to better rates or special arrangements not available online.

Contact Information for Booking

- **Booking Websites:**
  - [Booking.com](https://www.booking.com)
  - [Expedia](https://www.expedia.com)
  - [Airbnb](https://www.airbnb.com)

- **Local Travel Agencies:** Consider reaching out to local travel agencies for personalized recommendations and packages.

Chapter 11

Shopping and Souvenirs

Local Markets and Artisan Shops

Local markets are a great way to experience the culture of North Macedonia while picking up unique souvenirs and local products.

Skopje Old Bazaar (Stara Čaršija)
- **Description:** This historic bazaar dates back to the Ottoman era and is a vibrant area filled with narrow streets, shops, and cafes. Visitors can find a variety of goods, from handmade crafts to traditional clothing and spices.
- **Location:** Near the city center, Skopje.

- **Address:** Bazar, Skopje, North Macedonia.

Bitola Market
- **Description:** Bitola's central market offers fresh produce, traditional Macedonian products, and local delicacies. The market atmosphere is lively, with vendors selling fruits, vegetables, and homemade foods.
- **Location:** Central Bitola.
- **Address:** Trg 1 Maj, Bitola, North Macedonia.

Ohrid Marketplace
- **Description:** Located near Lake Ohrid, this market is known for its handicrafts, souvenirs, and fresh fish. Visitors can find traditional Macedonian woven goods, ceramics, and local snacks.
- **Location:** Near the Ohrid waterfront.
- **Address:** Market Square, Ohrid, North Macedonia.

Traditional Crafts and Products to Buy
North Macedonia is known for its rich tradition of handicrafts and artisanal products. Here are some must-buy items:

Macedonian Pottery
- **Description:** Handcrafted pottery, especially from the town of Ohrid, features intricate designs and bright colors. Traditional items include plates, bowls, and jugs.
- Where to Buy: Available in markets and specialized shops in Ohrid and Skopje.

Textiles and Embroidery

- **Description:** Traditional textiles, including handwoven carpets, tablecloths, and embroidered clothing, showcase the craftsmanship of local artisans. Look for the unique designs and patterns that represent Macedonian culture.
- **Where to Buy:** Local markets, shops in the Old Bazaar, Skopje, and artisan workshops in Tetovo.

Wine and Rakija
- **Description:** North Macedonia is known for its excellent wines and rakija (fruit brandy). Buying a bottle of local wine from Tikveš or a homemade rakija is a great way to take a piece of the culture home.
- **Where to Buy:** Local wineries, markets, and specialty shops in Skopje and Bitola.

Popular Shopping Streets and Centers

Several shopping areas in North Macedonia offer a mix of local and international brands, making them perfect for a leisurely shopping experience.

Macedonia Street (Makedonija)
- **Description:** Skopje's main shopping thoroughfare, Macedonia Street, features a mix of local shops, cafes, and international brands. It's a lively area that also includes several landmarks.
- **Location:** Starts from the City Square (Plostad Makedonija) and continues toward the Old Bazaar.
- **Address:** Macedonia Street, Skopje, North Macedonia.

City Mall Skopje

- **Description:** This modern shopping mall offers a variety of shops, restaurants, and entertainment options, including cinemas. It's a great spot to find both local and international brands.
- **Location:** Near the center of Skopje.
- **Address:** Blvd. 2, 1000 Skopje, North Macedonia.

Plaza Bitola
- **Description:** A popular shopping area in Bitola featuring a range of shops, cafes, and restaurants. Visitors can enjoy a pleasant walk while exploring local boutiques and souvenir shops.
- **Location:** In the heart of Bitola.
- **Address:** Shirok Sokak, Bitola, North Macedonia.

Skopje City Mall
- **Description:** Another major shopping destination in Skopje, this mall includes numerous retail stores, food options, and entertainment facilities, catering to diverse shopping needs.
- **Location:** Just outside the city center.
- **Address:** Blvd. 2, 1000 Skopje, North Macedonia.

Chapter 12

Culture, Festivals, and Local Etiquette

Customs and Traditions

North Macedonia is a country rich in customs and traditions influenced by its diverse history and cultural heritage.

Hospitality
- **Description:** Hospitality is a cornerstone of Macedonian culture. Guests are often welcomed with open arms, and it is customary to be offered food and drink upon entering a home. It is polite to accept these offerings, even if you are not hungry.

Traditional Greetings
- **Description:** A common greeting in Macedonia is "Zdravo" (Hello). When greeting, a handshake is standard for both men and women. Close friends may greet each other with a hug or a kiss on the cheek.

Religious Practices
- **Description:** The majority of North Macedonians are Orthodox Christians, and religious holidays play a significant role in daily life. Important customs include attending church services, lighting candles, and participating in feasts during religious holidays like Easter and Christmas.

Celebration of Name Days
- **Description:** Name days, which are associated with the feast days of saints, are celebrated similarly to birthdays. Friends and family often gather to celebrate, and it is customary for those celebrating to host guests.

Major Festivals and Events

North Macedonia hosts numerous festivals throughout the year, showcasing its rich cultural heritage, music, and traditions.

Ohrid Summer Festival
- **When:** July to August
- **Description:** This annual festival takes place in the picturesque city of Ohrid and features performances of classical music, opera, theater, and folklore. It attracts artists and visitors from around the world, making it a highlight of the cultural calendar.

Skopje Jazz Festival
- **When:** October
- **Description:** Celebrating jazz music, this festival attracts local and international musicians. It features concerts,

workshops, and jam sessions in various venues across Skopje, promoting jazz culture in the region.

Vardar Fest
- **When:** September
- **Description:** Held in the capital, Skopje, this festival celebrates traditional Macedonian music and dance. It showcases performances by local folk groups and promotes the preservation of national traditions.

Macedonian Wine Festival
- **When:** September
- **Description:** Celebrating the country's rich winemaking tradition, this festival features wine tastings, local food, and traditional music. It takes place in several cities, including Skopje and Bitola.

Art, Music, and Dance in Macedonian Culture

Art, music, and dance are integral to North Macedonia's cultural identity, with deep roots in history and tradition.

Traditional Music
- **Description:** Macedonian music is characterized by unique rhythms and melodies, often featuring traditional instruments like the tambura, gaida (bagpipe), and tapan (drum). Folk songs often reflect themes of love, nature, and historical events.

Folklore Dance
- **Description:** Traditional dances, such as the "oro," are performed at celebrations and festivals. These dances often involve intricate footwork and are typically performed in circles, showcasing community and unity.

Visual Arts
- **Description:** North Macedonian visual arts encompass various forms, from traditional embroidery and pottery to contemporary painting and sculpture. Icon painting, especially in Orthodox churches, is a notable aspect of the country's artistic heritage.

Etiquette Tips for Travelers
Understanding local etiquette will help you navigate social interactions smoothly during your visit to North Macedonia.

Dining Etiquette
- **Description:** If invited to someone's home, it's customary to bring a small gift, such as flowers or sweets. Wait for the host

to invite you to sit down before taking a seat at the table. During meals, it is polite to keep your hands on the table (but not your elbows).

Dress Code
- **Description:** Macedonians typically dress well for social occasions. In more rural areas, traditional clothing may still be worn during festivals and celebrations. It is advisable to dress modestly when visiting churches or religious sites.

Respect for Traditions
- **Description:** Always show respect for local customs and traditions. When visiting churches or participating in religious events, maintain a respectful demeanor and dress appropriately.

Photography Etiquette
- **Description:** Always ask for permission before photographing people, especially in rural areas or during private gatherings. Be mindful of cultural sensitivities regarding photography in religious sites.

Chapter 13

Practical Travel Tips and Final Essentials

Emergency Numbers and Health Services
Knowing the emergency numbers and healthcare facilities is crucial for a safe trip.

Emergency Numbers
- **Police:** 192
- **Ambulance:** 194
- **Fire Department:** 193
- **Emergency Services (General):** 112

Health Services
- **Hospitals and Clinics:** North Macedonia has both public and private healthcare facilities. Major cities like Skopje, Bitola, and Ohrid have hospitals that cater to various health needs.
    - **Clinical Center Skopje:** The largest hospital in North Macedonia, located in Skopje.
        - **Address:** 50, 1000 Skopje, North Macedonia.
        - **Phone:** +389 2 311 3277
    - **Hospital Bitola:** A regional hospital in Bitola.
        - **Address:** 17, 7000 Bitola, North Macedonia.

- **Phone:** +389 47 223 041
- **Private Clinics:** Numerous private clinics provide healthcare services in urban areas. These often offer shorter waiting times and English-speaking staff.

Travel Insurance
- It is highly recommended to have travel insurance that covers health emergencies, as healthcare costs can be significant for tourists without insurance.

Sustainable and Responsible Travel Advice

Traveling sustainably is vital to preserving North Macedonia's natural and cultural heritage.

Respect Local Culture
- **Engage with Locals:** Participate in local customs and traditions while being respectful. Understanding cultural norms enhances your experience.

Minimize Environmental Impact
- **Use Public Transport:** Utilize buses and other forms of public transport to reduce your carbon footprint. North Macedonia has an extensive and affordable public transport network.
- **Support Local Businesses:** Choose local eateries, markets, and artisans to support the economy and reduce environmental impact.

Leave No Trace

- When hiking or visiting natural sites, adhere to the "Leave No Trace" principles. Avoid littering and respect wildlife by keeping a safe distance.

Safety Tips for Travelers

While North Macedonia is generally safe for tourists, it's always wise to take precautions.

Stay Aware of Your Surroundings
- **Vigilance:** Be cautious in crowded areas, as pickpocketing can occur, especially in tourist hotspots. Keep your belongings secure and be aware of your surroundings.

Use Reputable Transportation
- **Taxis**: Use reputable taxi companies or rideshare apps to ensure safe transport. Avoid accepting rides from unmarked vehicles.

Keep Important Documents Safe
- **Documentation:** Keep copies of your passport, visa, and other important documents in a safe place. Store originals in a hotel safe.

Emergency Contacts
- Familiarize yourself with emergency contacts and the locations of nearby hospitals and police stations.

Useful Contacts: Tourist Centers, Embassies, and Consulates

Having the right contacts at hand can enhance your travel experience.

Tourist Information Centers
- Skopje Tourist Information Center
- **Location:** Near the city center at Macedonia Square.
- **Address:** Trg Makedonija 15, 1000 Skopje, North Macedonia.
- **Phone:** +389 2 310 1000

- Ohrid Tourist Information Center
- **Location:** Near the Ohrid waterfront.
- **Address:** Naum Ohridski 2, Ohrid, North Macedonia.
- **Phone:** +389 46 266 200

- Bitola Tourist Information Center
- **Location:** In the city center.
- **Address:** Shirok Sokak 56, Bitola, North Macedonia.
- **Phone:** +389 47 222 600

Embassies and Consulates
- U.S. Embassy
- **Address:** 1000 Skopje, North Macedonia.
- **Phone:** +389 2 311 0000

- British Embassy
- **Address:** 1000 Skopje, North Macedonia.
- **Phone:** +389 2 310 2000

- Australian Embassy
- **Address:** 1000 Skopje, North Macedonia.

- **Phone:** +389 2 310 2100

- **Canadian Embassy**
  - **Address:** 1000 Skopje, North Macedonia.
  - **Phone:** +389 2 310 3300

Conclusion

In conclusion, North Macedonia is a captivating destination that offers a rich tapestry of history, culture, and breathtaking landscapes. From the vibrant streets of Skopje to the serene shores of Lake Ohrid, every corner of this beautiful country tells a unique story waiting to be explored. As you wander through ancient ruins, savor traditional Macedonian cuisine, and immerse yourself in the warmth of local hospitality, you'll discover that North Macedonia is more than just a place to visit—it's an experience that lingers in your heart long after you leave. Whether you're seeking adventure, relaxation, or a deeper understanding of a culture that beautifully blends the old with the new, North Macedonia invites you to create unforgettable memories. So pack your bags, embrace the spirit of adventure, and let this hidden gem of the Balkans enchant you!

Feedback Request

Thank you for embarking on this journey through North Macedonia with my travel guide! I truly hope it has inspired you and helped prepare you for the unforgettable adventures that await in this remarkable country. Your feedback is incredibly valuable to me, and if you found the guide helpful, I'd be so grateful if you could take a moment to rate it. A positive review helps others discover this resource and ensures I can continue creating insightful and inspiring guides for travelers like you.

Your support means the world—happy travels, and I hope North Macedonia captures your heart just as it has mine!

Printed in Great Britain
by Amazon